OUTSMART!

OUTSMART!

HOW TO DO WHAT YOUR COMPETITORS CAN'T

JIM CHAMPY

© 2008 by Pearson Education, Inc.

Publishing as FT Press

Upper Saddle River, New Jersey 07458

Company and product names mentioned herein are the trademarks or registered trademarks of their respective owners.

Printed in the United States of America

First Printing March 2008

ISBN-10:   0-13-235777-1
ISBN-13:   978-0-13-235777-7

Pearson Education LTD.

Pearson Education Australia PTY, Limited.

Pearson Education Singapore, Pte. Ltd.

Pearson Education North Asia, Ltd.

Pearson Education Canada, Ltd.

Pearson Educatión de Mexico, S.A. de C.V.

Pearson Education—Japan

Pearson Education Malaysia, Pte. Ltd.

Library of Congress Cataloging-in-Publication Data

Champy, James, 1942-

   Outsmart! : how to do what your competitors can't / Jim Champy.

      p. cm.

   ISBN 0-13-235777-1 (hardback : alk. paper) 1. Competition--Handbooks, manuals, etc. 2. Success in business--Handbooks, manuals, etc. I. Title.

HD41.C463 2008

658.4'09--dc22

                    2007045693

Vice President, Publisher
Tim Moore

Associate Publisher and Director of Marketing
Amy Neidlinger

Editorial Assistant
Pamela Boland

Digital Marketing Manager
Julie Phifer

Marketing Coordinator
Megan Colvin

Cover Designer
Ingredient

Managing Editor
Gina Kanouse

Senior Project Editor
Kristy Hart

Copy Editor
Krista Hansing
Editorial Services

Senior Indexer
Cheryl Lenser

Interior Designer
Ingredient

Senior Compositor
Jake McFarland

Manufacturing Buyer
Dan Uhrig

This book is dedicated to my father,
who was my first teacher in business.

CONTENTS

ABOUT THE AUTHOR

Jim Champy is one of the leading management and business thinkers of our time. His first best seller, *Reengineering the Corporation*, remains the bible for executing process change. His second book, *Reengineering Management*, another best seller, was recognized by *Business Week* as one of the most important books of its time. But Champy is also an experienced manager and advisor. He is the Chairman of Consulting for Perot Systems. He speaks and writes with the authority of real business experience and brings pragmatism to the world of business. In this new series of books, Champy looks at what's working today for high-growth businesses. Champy observes that there is not much new in management, but there is a lot new in business—and a lot to learn from what's new.

IN MY MORE THAN 30 YEARS OF
WORK AS A CONSULTANT AND
AUTHOR, I'VE LEARNED THAT THE
BEST IDEAS ARE FOUND INSIDE
COMPANIES. BUT IT WASN'T ALWAYS
SO. THERE WAS A TIME WHEN
I STRAYED FROM THE REALM
OF HANDS-ON PRAGMATISM
TO SEARCH THE WRITINGS OF
PHILOSOPHERS FOR IDEAS THAT
COULD BE APPLIED TO BUSINESS.
TO BE HONEST, I THOUGHT THAT
QUOTING THE ANCIENTS MADE ME
SOUND SMARTER.

INTRODUCTION

One day, while waxing philosophic during a speech in Monterey, Mexico, I encountered a far smarter gentleman of a certain age sitting in the front row. He interrupted me to ask how the philosophy of Mexico's nineteenth-century ruler, Gen. Antonio Santa Anna, could be applied to management. What could a man both admired and reviled contribute to business? The answer, which my interlocutor duly shared with all present, was a gem of pragmatism. Santa Anna, he told us, firmly believed that whatever worked was the right thing to do.

I have taken his lesson to heart, and this book describes the very real and practical strategies that are working for today's most successful businesses, strategies that I believe will sustain their success into the future. Because the primary goal of all good strategy is growth, the companies analyzed in these pages are among the world's fastest-growing enterprises.

But equally important, their revenue-producing ideas are neither hypothetical nor based on esoteric technologies. They don't require hundreds of millions of venture capital dollars or the vast sums from stock offerings to implement. Rather, they are strategies that any business leader can easily and immediately understand.

This is the first in a planned series comprising four compact volumes on the key topics of strategy, marketing, leadership, and operations. Taken together, the books aim to deliver the most current intelligence available on how to succeed in today's brave new world of business. An ambitious objective? Yes. But what I see a host of companies accomplishing today has me both excited and encouraged.

My ability to write about these matters does not derive from scholarly pursuits, although I've braved assorted academic challenges. Necessity drove me to learn by doing. It is a path that I recommend to anyone who seeks a powerful curriculum and an unforgettable teacher.

In my younger years, I assumed that I would join my family's construction business in Lawrence, Massachusetts, a mill city north of Boston. My quest for relevant knowledge sent me to the Massachusetts Institute of Technology (MIT), where I studied engineering, then to Boston College where I studied law. Finally, I returned to Lawrence for my early training in business.

In my family's company, there were no strategies, business plans, or budgets. We did what seemed right—day by day. We hired people, bought equipment—even acquired real estate—that seemed good for the business. Risk taking was a natural act. We had no spreadsheets, and the most advanced form of technology was a mechanical calculator. But the business worked—most of the time.

In Lawrence, I also had my first taste of a multicultural world. We had stone masons from Italy, carpenters from Quebec, and painters from Ireland. I learned a lot from these folks— something about teams, but more about how, when left alone, good people will do the right thing. I carried this and other lessons into my life in business.

Thanks to my MIT roommate, Tom Gerrity, I was later treated to an advanced course in commerce when he invited two MIT friends and me to join him in a business venture. In 1969, we launched Index Systems, an information-technology start-up based on Tom's Ph.D. research into automating management decision making. We each invested $370, the bet of a lifetime. Because our work was on the cutting edge of technology and business change, we serendipitously became an acquisition target for a bigger company nearly two decades later. In 1988, Computer Science Corporation (CSC) bought our firm and turned it into CSC's management-consulting arm. I became CSC Index's CEO and chairman after the Wharton School of Business lured away our hottest property, Tom, to become the school's dean. I was left to expand CSC Index into what became a $240 million company.

Out of those Index years came the ideas—developed with Michael Hammer and other colleagues—that formed my first book, *Reengineering the Corporation,* which argued that companies need to change radically and be managed from a process perspective. It became the best-selling business book of the 1990s. I followed this with a second book, *Reengineering Management,* in which I contended that leaders had to change their own ways of thinking before they could change their organizations. And in a third book, *X-Engineering the Corporation,* I made the case that process change must extend outside company walls to suppliers, customers, and business partners.

My current job as Chairman of Consulting for Perot Systems gives me access to many leaders who live and work on the frontiers of business, where the rules of industry are stretched (and sometimes broken). What I learn from these leaders is what I teach to others, and I write books to crystallize the findings of my latest field research.

My best work, however, has always been done with collaborators. And for this book, and the three that will follow in this series, I must acknowledge and thank the talented editors and researchers at Wordworks, Inc.—Donna Sammons Carpenter, Maurice Coyle, Ruth Hlavacek, Larry Martz, Molly Sammons Morris, Cindy Sammons, Robert Shnayerson, Robert W. Stock, and Ellen Wojahn; and Helen Rees and Joan Mazmanian of the Helen Rees Literary Agency. I would also like to acknowledge my very able assistant, Dee Dee Haggerty. And, as always, I am grateful to my wife, Lois, and my son, Adam, for their support, advice, and tolerance when I write. Lois and Adam keep me grounded.

Nothing pleases me more than sharing what we have discovered with people who might actually use it, especially when the ideas we have uncovered are not only fresh, but simple and practical. Ahead lies a world of creative companies with uncommon strategies and a singular record for making good on them. How do they do it?

I HAVE ALWAYS ADMIRED
CHARLES DARWIN, NOT LEAST
BECAUSE HE NEVER ALLOWED
FAITH, INTUITION, OR RECEIVED
WISDOM TO BLIND HIM TO FACT.
HE DIDN'T JUST HANG AROUND
HIS OFFICE TOUTING UNPROVEN
THEORIES. INSTEAD HE
TRAVELED FAR AFIELD IN SEARCH
OF ACTUAL EXPERIENCE AND
MADE DETAILED OBSERVATIONS.
HE WAS BENT ON TESTING HIS
THEORIES TO FIND OUT WHAT
REALLY WORKED.

CHAPTER 1
IT'S A SMART, SMART,
SMART, SMART WORLD

Darwin grew up surrounded by Victorian England's certainties, among them that God created the world and all its creatures (especially Englishmen) in seven days. And it was considered a near certainty that young Charles would follow his father and grandfather into medicine. That idea collapsed: Charles had no interest in the family business, nor in his father's fallback plan to educate his son as an Anglican clergyman, in those days a highly respected and fairly well-paid calling. Instead Charles chose to sail the world, collecting hundreds of animal and plant specimens. What he discovered raised hard questions about God's authorship and introduced a whole new vision of the way the world works.

Darwin's 1859 volume, *On the Origin of Species,* proposed an evolution scenario that has guided scientists ever since. Supported by vast research, as well as his personal

ρ **Charles Darwin**
(February 1809 – April 1882)

After becoming eminent among scientists for his field work and inquiries into geology, he proposed and provided scientific evidence that all species of life have evolved over time from one or a few common ancestors through the process of natural selection.

observations as an avid pigeon fancier and breeder, Darwin made three declarations:

1. Species always breed beyond available resources.

2. Those with favorable variations have a greater chance of survival and pass on their variations to their offspring.

3. Adapted species force out weaker ones, producing whole new species.

So that's life, real life—one, two, three. In the unending, tooth-and-claw competition, only the fittest survive.

This book is about real business life—namely, outsmarting the competition. Darwin has a lot to teach. As he might put it, businesses breed beyond available customers; companies with successful strategies have a better chance of survival; and successful enterprises force out weaker ones, creating whole new business models. In other words, the businesses that succeed not only survive, but grow, gaining more of the supply of customers and forcing their rivals to adapt or die.

DARWIN HAS A LOT TO TEACH. AS HE MIGHT PUT IT, BUSINESSES BREED BEYOND AVAILABLE CUSTOMERS; COMPANIES WITH SUCCESSFUL STRATEGIES HAVE A BETTER CHANCE OF SURVIVAL; AND SUCCESSFUL ENTERPRISES FORCE OUT WEAKER ONES, CREATING WHOLE NEW BUSINESS MODELS.

I usually don't write about my own failures as a consultant, but this is a good place to recall a client of mine who was saved from extinction only by an acquisitive competitor. In the late 1990s, the venerable European airline, Swiss Air, was threatened by the rise of British Air and Lufthansa; both had more routes and more ways to spread costs. Swiss Air asked me for advice on survival tactics. I concluded that the company could no longer compete simply by staying aloft. But it still owned all sorts of ground assets—hotels, duty-free shops, an advanced ticketing system, and significant control over Swiss airports. Why not reinvent Swiss Air as a truly friendly carrier focused on improving the entire travel experience? I urged its leaders to integrate all its assets and compete anew as Europe's first total air-travel company, featuring complete service from the ground up, as it were.

ρ **Swiss Air**

Swiss Air emerged from bankruptcy as simply "Swiss." The airline still operates under that brand, even though it was acquired by Lufthansa. A respected small airline, Swiss struggled against its larger competitors. The question now: How will Lufthansa leverage the Swiss brand?

Swiss Air's executives balked. My notion violated their traditional thinking. For airline industry managers—in those days, anyway—competing centered on adding new routes and dishing out edible food onboard. Hotel- and shop-keeping were just not part of their flight plans. So Swiss Air ignored my advice and bought interests in other European airlines, hoping to expand routes and capture customers from its rivals. Unfortunately, it bought into cash-poor carriers whose heavy borrowing eventually drove Swiss Air into bankruptcy. Lufthansa picked up the company for a song in 2002. So much for the wisdom of clinging to a defunct image in a world that couldn't care less.

In the end, Swiss Air, unable to escape its outdated perceptions, lost its independence and slightly tarnished the Swiss Cross. I still fly the airline from time to time as a matter of choice, and I think about what might have been or whether the company was destined to be overtaken by one of its European rivals. In some businesses, as this book makes clear, scale does play an important role.

AT HIGH ALTITUDES, EVEN THE SMARTEST COMPANIES ARE NOT IMMUNE TO DIZZINESS AND GROUPTHINK.

At the other extreme of Darwinian cautionary tales are the supersuccessful big corporations that succumb to hubris and begin overreaching. Embodying another form of adaptive failure, they throw caution to the winds and plunge ahead with what's been called a moon shot, typically some highly hyped new product that fails in the marketplace. A recent example is the Segway. At high altitudes, even the smartest companies are not immune to dizziness and groupthink.

"CHAOS IS AN OPPORTUNITY"

My anecdotes gain greater meaning when placed in a larger context: the unprecedented dynamism of world capitalism today. Change is the very essence of business, of course—hence, its Darwinian imperatives. But nothing in the past compares with the speed and profundity of business changes in the early twenty-first century. Barring some worrisome exceptions, business-growth trends point sharply upward. Across the globe, opportunity is in the saddle. We live in a time of innovation and expansion—a world of smart and smarter strategic options, as the title of this chapter suggests. The catch is that the prize will go to the smartest competitor: In whatever field you're playing, you must outsmart all your rivals. But luckily, the world is expanding rapidly. Shrewd competitors can stake out new territory, define the boundaries, and even set new rules for the game.

My friend Peter Drucker, the late, great management thinker, was famous for declaring in the fairly peaceful 1980s, "Chaos is an opportunity, not a threat." Good minds may differ on whether chaos describes the twenty-first century. But if this century is defined by an endless torrent of problems that people will pay anything to solve, then we live in promising times. The problems (a.k.a. opportunities) begin with the immense impact

ρ Peter Drucker
I had the privilege of having Peter as a friend and adviser. We shared speaking engagements from time to time. Often, he would take a half hour to answer a question, because he liked to set the answer in its historical context. In my opinion, he was the great business pragmatist of the last century.

ρ Delhi, India
I travel to India three times a year on business. The quality of talent is exceptional, but the country's infrastructure is challenging at best. Still, it is nothing short of inspiring to see the country's emerging middleclass. India, from my point of view, is both an enormous source of talent and an enormous, developing market.

of ever more humans seeking better lives on a planet whose size is fixed.

According to the McKinsey Global Institute, over the next 10 years, nearly 450 million newcomers will join the middle class in China and India alone. The drive for a better life in emerging countries has created huge new markets for low-cost housing and building materials, for amenities ranging from cell phones to detergents, and for new public facilities such as hospitals and airports. In July 2007, Boeing unveiled its new 787 jetliner (capacity: 210 to 330 passengers, depending on the model), with a record 634 orders already firmly booked, mainly from airlines serving emerging countries.

Only 15 years ago, the world's total gross domestic product (GDP) was $13 billion; now it's $65.95 trillion. Major American

companies are scrambling to keep up with the rising economic clout of Brazil, China, India, and Russia. In a recent nine-month flurry, Goldman Sachs's chief executive, Lloyd Blankfein, opened more new offices than ever—in Dubai, Qatar, Moscow, Mumbai, Sao Paulo, and Tel Aviv. In a day when General Electric (GE) is growing twice as fast outside the United States as at home, its CEO, Jeffrey Immelt, spends three months a year traveling abroad to garner even more emerging-market business.

Not that GE is hurting at home. Developed countries are doing well. But the big global story is that former have-nots are surging even faster in population and prosperity. Since 1998, GDP per capita in the developing world has risen by 4.5 percent a year, twice the rate of the so-called advanced economies.

ρ **Dubai**

In infrastructure, the Middle East more than makes up for what India lacks. These countries aspire to be the number one place where business is done, and they are investing heavily to turn that dream into a reality.

⌕ **Cash**

As credit tightens, cash becomes more important—and many large corporations have lots of money on their balance sheets. Investors need to allow companies to use that cash to improve their businesses, rather than just returning money to shareholders as dividends.

Is all this global prosperity simply another boom-driven delusion masking the inevitable bust lying in wait? Yes, no, maybe—take your pick. Whatever happens, the world will keep turning. The great economist Paul Samuelson was once asked what would happen if a great monetary crisis, then looming, actually happened. "The sun will come up tomorrow," he said, "and the bridges will continue to bear the traffic." It took me years to grasp his message: In any conditions, business keeps going—and the winners will outsmart the losers and keep growing.

In summer 2007, for example, governments and gurus hailed the world's economic health. Credit ruled; liquidity abounded. Investors splurged on ever-rising equities; bargain hunters snapped up shaky businesses, leveraging everything on the road to El Dorado. The world was awash with easy money.

Then, suddenly, it dried up. Billions upon billions of subprime mortgage debt had been sliced and diced like so much sausage meat, and pieces of it were sold and resold to ever more remote holders at questionably high prices. Finally, no one knew what its real worth was and prices plummeted. At that point, trust vanished, credit of all kinds evaporated, and central banks poured billions of dollars of reserves into the financial system, hoping to prevent a total credit collapse. Nevertheless, the crunch radiated outward, alarming not only mortgage-debt holders, but corporate shareholders as well. Fearful of losing recent gains, millions of former equity buyers abruptly switched from euphoria to escape mode, causing big stock sell-offs on bourses from Beijing to New York. British bankers shuddered at a sight unseen since the Great Depression: a classic run on a bank, with lines of depositors clamoring for their money outside the mortgage lender Northern Rock in spite of the British Treasury's promise to bail out any banks in trouble.

A world heady with options had suddenly glimpsed the reverse—a potentially bleak future of shriveled lending, stalled expansion, bankruptcies, and unemployment.

The upshot of all this ferment is that business has never been more complex, volatile, and demanding, yet so full of opportunity. Technological advances in a world made flat have spawned a time of almost hyperbolic risk and reward. So we pursue the old grail of competitive advantage with powerful new weapons: high-velocity concepts, unprecedented products, and sophisticated marketing tools. The combat is unforgiving, the casualties unremitting.

In fact, the business world has become a great dynamo of
fascinating new practices that can sharpen any company's
competitive edge. That's why I often say that there is not much
new in management. But there is a lot new in business. And
much of what's new in business today has to do with the strategy
needed for growth, the goal of any successful business. I can
testify that the new trends in strategy bear no resemblance to
the days when haughty executives joined outside consultants for
meditations on the future while golfing on plush green courses.

THAT'S WHY I OFTEN SAY THAT THERE'S NOTHING NEW IN MANAGEMENT, BUT THERE'S MUCH NEW IN BUSINESS.

Exciting change is underway. Sure, a lot of companies haven't
gotten the message and are still doing business the same
old way—I call them "incumbents," like lazy politicians sure
of being reelected. But sooner or later, if they don't wise up,
the incumbents will get an unpleasant surprise from a smart
company like the ones I've observed. In their offices, the
obsessive Captain Queeg–like CEOs of yesterday are gone.
Their successors realize that big egos produce big problems;
they welcome the bracing truth that strategy is best shaped by
a company's collective wisdom, not by the occupants of the
executive suite alone. Strategy rises organically from whatever
happens on the front lines and everywhere in between. Hence,
my exemplary companies are outsmarting and outgrowing
their competitors by finding distinctive market positions
and sustainable advantages in all kinds of ways—whether it's
thinking innovatively, simplifying complex problems for their
customers, or finding ways to tap into the success of others.

WINNERS IN THE GROWTH RACE

Research for this book has been rigorous and far reaching. In Darwinian mode, I have collected specimen companies and analyzed their successes, pinpointing the methods by which they unarguably beat their competitors. I began with the premise that any company growing by more than 15 percent a year for the past three or more years had to be pursuing a notable strategy.

The facts were even more stunning: My colleagues and I actually spotted a few businesses growing at phenomenal rates of more than 5,000 percent a year. This exercise yielded a total of 1,000 high-velocity businesses with growth rates above 15 percent, enough to keep us toiling for the next 20 years. We began winnowing this down to a more manageable number and conducting extensive personal interviews with company leaders. It turned out that some of the candidates with exceptional growth rates weren't being driven by their strategies; they were just lucky, or riding a trend. The finalists were a fascinating lot, creative companies with unusual strategies that, as noted in the Introduction, combined an irresistible promise to customers with an enviable record for delivering it.

The rest of this book is a series of short studies describing these fast-growth companies and the often counterintuitive practices their leaders have used to outsmart the competition—and get better at what they do. Here's a quick rundown of the businesses and the uncommonly smart leaders I want you to meet:

▶ Panos Panay was a guitarist who never made it but a
talent agent who did—and he never forgot how tough it
is for hungry musicians to connect with the promoters
who might hire them. No talent agency can afford to do
that job—the commissions are too small. Then Panos had
an idea. As set forth in Chapter 2, "Compete by Seeing
What Others Don't: How Sonicbids Spotted a $15 Billion
Market," he created Sonicbids, where promoters—10,000
of them, at last count—can list the events for which they
need musicians, and the 120,000 musician-members can
look over the list and make their contacts. Sonicbids also
helps members prepare electronic press kits that they
can easily and rapidly e-mail to promoters. Though the
individual gigs are small, they are huge in the aggregate;
the annual payout for wedding bands, for example, is $2.5
billion. That's only one of the very promising markets
Panos is now pursuing, thanks to his knack for recognizing
an opportunity that no one else saw.

▶ After an exasperating emergency-room experience
with his son, Rick Krieger came up with an idea: a kiosk
staffed by a nurse practitioner to handle those common
medical problems—say, a sinus infection, strep throat,
or an allergy—that don't need a doctor's expertise. Mike
Howe had the retailing smarts to shape the idea and
give it a national footprint. In Chapter 3, "Compete by
Thinking Outside the Bubble: MinuteClinic Delivers
Healthcare Retail," you will read how the company known
as MinuteClinic has evolved despite all sorts of challenges.
It's a powerful example of how borrowing an idea from
a seemingly unrelated industry can be a great way to
outsmart your competitors.

▶ Smith & Wesson was 155 years old and nearly dead. Sales and the stock price had plummeted, and federal agents were looking into accounting problems. But instead of administering last rites, CEO Mike Golden dosed the gun company with powerful medicine: his own rebranding expertise. He knew nothing about the weapons business— he'd never fired a gun in his life—but he had learned all about brand management at the Kohler Company and marketing at Black & Decker, where, Golden quips, employees "did hand-to-hand combat at the retail level." Chapter 4, "Compete by Using All You Know: Basics Are Blazing at Smith & Wesson," demonstrates that nothing beats the impact of a driven CEO determined to apply his personal savvy.

▶ In the beginning, Shutterfly was just an online photo finisher. Then Jeffrey Housenbold became chief executive and brought with him a far grander vision of the company. He saw it as being at the nexus of a new era in the worlds of photography and communication. Within a couple of years, he transformed it into a community united by a love of photographs and their power to capture family memories. Chapter 5, "Compete by Changing Your Frame of Reference: How Shutterfly Saw the Bigger Picture," shows how Jeff worked his magic at Shutterfly. His wide-lens vision, combined with a finely honed sense of people's ever-growing need to connect, helped Jeff reimagine the company as a social-expression business. Now two million members trade experiences and feelings as well as photos. They buy not only Shutterfly's photo-printing services, but everything from calendars to scrapbooks, to posters and more.

▶ "From concept to creation" is the mantra at S.A. Robotics of Loveland, Colorado. The maker of custom robotic arms and lifting devices goes to great lengths—literally, up to 100 feet (the size of some of its robots)—to prevent humans from coming into contact with nuclear waste, lethal chemicals, and other dangerous substances. The robots, which cost between $1 million and $2 million apiece, are selling as fast as S.A. Robotics's 140 satisfied employees can make them. The turnover rate at the company is nearly zero, while its annual growth rate is a whopping 70 percent. Chapter 6, "Compete by Doing Everything Yourself: S.A. Robotics—Reaching Into Every Detail," examines how the company's decision to do in-house design, engineering, testing, and manufacturing has enabled it to leap ahead of its competitors to capture contracts from around the world.

▶ Have you ever noticed how a product, new or old, can suddenly take on such cachet that it gains almost cultlike status among certain groups of consumers? Chapter 7, "Compete by Tapping the Success of Others: Jibbitz Wins by Riding a Croc," recounts the stories of Jeff Grady and Sheri and Rick Schmelzer, who made their fortunes by developing accessories for two such must-have items. Jeff found his niche accessorizing the iPod after Apple failed to provide consumers with protective cases for their beloved gadgets. The Schmeltzers' story is the same but different: They accessorized the popular Crocs' molded plastic clogs, customizing the ubiquitous footwear with their Jibbitz decorations. So smart was their strategy that Crocs wanted to be part of it, so it bought Jibbitz and kept the Schmeltzers on to run it.

▶ I've never understood why appliance manufacturers and retailers of consumer durables can't find a better way of getting the parts customers need for their washers/ dryers, television sets, refrigerators, and the like. Finding the right person to talk to when you need, say, an ice-maker bucket or a remote control is always a hassle, with customers bouncing from retailer to distributor to manufacturer. Then they have to wait weeks for the new part to arrive—weeks without a crucial appliance. That was the aggravating system that Partsearch set out to fix. Chapter 8, "Compete by Creating Order Out of Chaos: Partsearch Finds the Item You Need," describes how Glenn Laumeister put together a catalog of eight million parts and accessories encompassing more than 560 brands.

▶ Some of the great business success stories of our time are built on a three-word strategy for corralling customers: Keep it simple. No one wants to buy a product or service that's so complicated that it's hard or even dangerous to use. When Becky Minard discovered that her beloved horse Westley was not getting the supplements the veterinarian had ordered, she wanted to know why. The answer: The method used to deliver and distribute supplements at horse barns was impossibly complex and invited error. Becky and her husband developed a technique for packaging supplements and medications that has evolved into a $40 million company called SmartPak. Naturally, it wasn't easy. As H. L. Mencken memorably noted, "For every complex problem, there is a solution that is simple, neat, and wrong." But as Chapter 9, "Compete by Simplifying Complexity: SmartPak Brings Stability to the Stables," shows, this couple found a way to build a thriving business by keeping it simple.

These vignettes might already have you thinking about how
you will apply the lessons from these companies to your own.
It won't be simple; each example in this book is unique, and
none of these companies has a formula you can follow without
changes to how you operate. But these companies do share
some characteristics. First, they follow Drucker's simple advice
to know where you are, where you want to be, and how to get
there, and that approach blurs the traditional line between
strategy and execution. In almost everything they've done,
the people you will meet in these pages have carved out paths
that are both distinctive and competitive. Their search for the
future has opened their eyes to opportunities that others have
overlooked and led them to places where others have not dared
to go. And in making the journey, they have found the holy grail
of strategy: an unmet customer need.

Outsmarting the competition requires more than intelligence,
experience, and business sense; you also have to be quick,
flexible, and ready to adapt to the transforming world. The
penalty for failure is Darwinian extinction, but the prize for
success is survival, growth, and the rich rewards of a life spent
in the brave new world of business. As you read each of the
following chapters, keep your mind open to new ways of seeing
and doing.

Taken together, the companies that you are about to meet
represent what is really working in business today. They have a
lot to teach us.

IN AN ERA WHEN OUR CELEBRITY-
OBSESSED SOCIETY HANGS ON EVERY
WORD AND DEED—BOTH GOOD
AND BAD—OF A HANDFUL OF HOT
PROPERTIES, IT'S EASY TO FORGET
THAT HUNDREDS OF THOUSANDS
OF TALENTED ARTISTS GO ALMOST
UNNOTICED. FOR THESE MUSICIANS,
SINGERS, ACTORS, MAGICIANS, AND
THE LIKE, GETTING NOTICED AND
GETTING WORK IS AN ARDUOUS
TASK. BUT THANKS TO BOSTON
ENTREPRENEUR PANOS PANAY
AND HIS COMPANY, THEIR STRUGGLE
MIGHT COME TO AN END.

CHAPTER 2

Compete by Seeing What Others Don't: How Sonicbids Spotted a $15 Billion Market

Not long ago, I had the chance to sit down with the 35-year-old Panay in Boston's South End. Sonicbids, the business he founded and serves as the chief executive of, ranks 88th on *Inc.* magazine's list of the top 5,000 privately owned businesses in the United States. Launched in 2001, Sonicbids had revenue of $248,000 in 2003, $3 million in 2005, and $8 million in 2007. With growth like that, I thought, he must have a special understanding of what it takes to create and run a business in today's ever more competitive environment. He does.

Panay is, by all accounts, an intelligent, empathetic, forceful leader—and he also has a knack for spotting markets everyone else has neglected and then figuring out how to serve them efficiently and profitably. He describes himself as an intuitive thinker, one who connects dots of information that form a bigger picture most people fail to see.

ρ **Sonicbids**
The brilliance of Sonicbids' approach to business is that it gives every band an international stage, even those that started—and stayed—in a garage.

ρ **Wedding**
Did you know that weddings—and other such events—are a $15 billion dollar market? But it's a market that was waiting to be aggregated. It took the ubiquity of information technology to enable that to take place.

Panay was already a top executive at a major talent agency when he spotted a huge opportunity: Because the big agents are interested in representing only established stars who bring in large fees, fully nine-tenths of the $15 billion annual business of connecting promoters with musicians needed for temporary gigs was being served in catch-as-catch-can fashion. Making use of technology, Panay figured out how to connect thousands of aspiring musicians and small bands with promoters who needed their talents. He christened his brainchild Sonicbids.

Most talent agents collect a fee equivalent to just 10 percent of their clients' earnings, so they see it as a waste of time and energy to book, say, a wedding band that gets only $800 for a night's work or a low-paying engagement in a small club or coffeehouse. But Panay saw otherwise. The wedding band business by itself totals $2.5 billion, plus there's another $11 billion in bookings at

small bars, clubs, coffeehouses, festivals, colleges, and private parties. And Panay adds, "We've got lots of room to grow."

Sonicbids is akin to a musical matchmaker that works both sides of the aisle but prods its musicians to show their best face to suitors. It takes no commissions from its musicians, charging them only a membership fee of $50 to $100 a year. They receive help putting together an electronic press kit (EPK) that includes an MP3 sample of their music, photos, biographical material, and press clippings. EPKs simplify the promotional process and are cheaper than creating and mailing multiple physical press kits. The EPKs can then be submitted online to one or more of the promoters listed on the site who are actively looking for artists to hire.

Some 10,000 promoters use the site to connect with Sonicbids' 120,000 musician members, a quarter of whom are from abroad. The site facilitates connections via a community forum and an advanced search tool that enables members to narrow their quest by location, date, and genre. Promoters charge Sonicbids' members anywhere from a few dollars to $25 to submit an EPK but agree, as part of their contract with Sonicbids, that they will actually review all the submissions they receive. The submission fee, which is far lower than the commission a musician would have to pay an ordinary booking agent, helps to ensure that members send their EPKs only when they have a realistic shot at landing a performance. It also prevents promoters from being flooded with applications.

Panay was born and raised on the Mediterranean island of
Cyprus. Hoping to become the next George Benson, a legendary
jazz guitarist, he enrolled at Boston's Berklee College of Music
in 1991. "Thankfully, I found out in time that I wasn't good
enough," he told me. He then decided to take courses in the
music business. Peter Spellman, director of Berklee's career
development center, recalls that, while still a student, Panay
"organized one of the best-produced international tours for a
Berklee artist" that Spellman had ever seen.

After college, Panay became an intern, then an agent, and
eventually a vice president in the international division of Ted
Kurland Associates, the large and influential Boston-based
artist booking and management company. For almost seven
years, he represented some of the world's best-known musical
figures, many of whom he had admired while growing up.
Working with artists like Pat Metheny, Chick Corea, Sonny
Rollins, Branford Marsalis, and Al Di Meola "was a real blast,"
he told me, "and I learned the value of doing something that
you love."

Then came the day nearly eight years ago when Panay picked
up a book called *Blur.* The author contended that the wired
world was eliminating the lines between traditional business
categories. What sparked Panay's imagination, in particular,
though, was the suggestion that once-separate products
and services were blending on the Internet. That nugget of
knowledge inspired Panay to come up with the concept of
Sonicbids, a vehicle he conceived as both product and service
that would connect promoters and aspiring musicians with a
minimum of fuss and bother. Panay was on his way to totally

uncovering a market that everyone else had overlooked, and he would develop a whole new business model to profit from it.

Panay constructed his intuitive big picture from myriad factual dots, most of them denoting dysfunctions. "I remember when I first started as an agent," he told me, "getting buried under press kits from musicians who wanted to get booked by me, but I never had time to listen to their tapes and CDs." As Panay fought the deluge, he knew that musicians trying to make a living at their trade languished in endless frustration. They had to await the preparation of an elaborate press kit, mail the kit to talent agents or promoters, spend anxious weeks and months waiting for a response, call around to make sure the kits had even arrived (let alone been reviewed), and perhaps bear the misery of another rejection or no response at all.

All through the years, Panay kept thinking there had to be a better way. And once he came up with the idea for Sonicbids, he couldn't sit still. Within a few months, he quit his job and began putting together a business plan. He turned his apartment into a home office, maxed out his credit cards, and used up his life savings. Finally, after receiving financing help from family and friends, he created Sonicbids and opened for business in 2001.

Initially, he hoped the site would serve as a trusted third party through which promoters could find a band, make an offer, and pay the band. That was the concept that led him to name his company Sonicbids. In short order, though, he realized he would have to create a sense of trust within a large community of musicians and promoters before he could successfully put his model in place. That's when he turned to his current arrangement, in which the promoters pay the musicians directly.

Panay's experience as an agent helped him to avoid a pitfall that has engulfed other entrepreneurs trying to tap the same market. He knew better than to spend time and resources trying to attract musicians to sign up for his services. "Artists are already the proactive party," he explains. "The promoter is more passive. His problem isn't that he has to go fishing for musicians. It's how to deal with the slew of musicians who are trying to connect with him. So I realized my first goal was to attract the promoter to the site. If that worked, the musicians would find their way."

The lure he dangled before promoters was the chance to simplify the task of finding an artist, do it free of charge, and, in effect, get paid for it by charging the artists submission

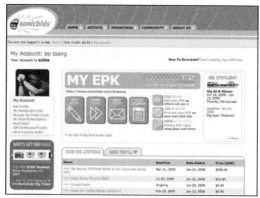

© Sonicbids. Reprinted with permission.

fees. Here's how Panay's model works. A promoter who lists a gig on Sonicbids can log into his or her account and see a relatively manageable list of artists applying for the job. They have read the job description, including the time and location, the type of music desired, and the pay being offered. They have paid the promoter's required submission fee, a process that tends to weed out musicians who send out press kits indiscriminately to hundreds of events. The promoter can then quickly check out the EPKs, listen to some music, read any special notes an artist may have added, and decide whether the artist is a match.

One of the intangibles Panay offers both the promoters and the musicians is a proactive customer-service operation, which is, in effect, the character and personality of the business. "One of the problems you have in an online business," he explains, "is that you don't have a physical presence, like a restaurant where people can walk in and smell and touch. You don't have that kind of legitimacy by virtue of where you exist. We try to make up for that by the language we use, the way we communicate." The people who answer the phones are young and sympathetic to customers' needs, particularly those of struggling young musicians. Aware of their insecurity, Panay insists that the musicians be treated respectfully. There is a standing rule, for example, that e-mails must be answered the same day they are received.

Panay also insists that his 50 employees listen to what the customers say about Sonicbids and report back what they hear. He learned that the hard way, by failing to check with the Sonicbids community before introducing a feedback mechanism to the site. Panay thought that the artists would enjoy and benefit from hearing what they all had to say about each other. Unfortunately, too many of the comments were negative, and sometimes Member A would post snide remarks about Member B if the two were competing for a gig. The feedback caused an uproar and a load of cancellations. "People were freaking out," Panay recalls. "I think it was the first time I felt my instincts had failed me."

To balance his own intuitive approach, Panay now consciously seeks out employees who are strong analytically. "I try not to hire clones of me because I don't feel you build a great team that way," he says. He also relies on a continuous infusion of new facts and ideas, seeking to upgrade and reinvent himself. "You've got to continuously use information to refine your instincts," he told me. He constantly asks people at work and elsewhere to explain things to him. "You're the boss, but you have to assume the person you hired knows how to do their job better than you'd ever do it," he says. "So I ask them to tell me what something means or how a process works. Bosses need a little humility."

"You've got to continuously use information to refine your instincts."

While refining his role as Sonicbids' leader, Panay is also aware of the need to keep honing his team. "The thinking you're using and the team you're using to get you to a particular point are certainly not going to get you to the point after that," he says. And for a chief executive who hopes to convert Sonicbids into a billion-dollar business, there are bound to be challenges ahead.

"Growing a company sounds a lot easier in the media than in real life," Panay acknowledges. "It's kind of like the story of the singer who gets discovered in a smoky bar and becomes Barbra Streisand. People like these rags-to-riches stories, but nobody talks about all the tough work that goes into an artist's training—or into the Google or eBay successes, either."

Panay has proved both his capacity for difficult work and his ability to see what others don't. As he expands his vision and plans for the next stage of his business, he expects to offer his members the kind of payment security that Panay, as talent agent, once provided for the big-name stars. For artists who made around $30,000 a night, he would handle the booking and the promoter would wire him 50 percent of the fee to be placed in an escrow account. That way, the artists knew they were guaranteed to receive at least half their contracted amount if the promoter reneged in any way. And the promoter, in turn, knew he wasn't going to lose that money if a performer failed to show.

As Panay envisions it, his site will perform the same service for bands making, say, $1,000 a night. If the musicians don't appear or can't play for some other reason, the promoter will get his money back. But if all goes well, the band will get $500 from the promoter after the show on top of the $500 in the escrow account, which will be transferred into the band's Sonicbids account—minus a small fee for the service. In addition, the site will allow artists and promoters to rate each other, similar to the eBay and Amazon ratings, following a performance. But ever mindful of his feedback fiasco, Panay promises that the ratings will be vetted before they go up on the site.

Panay also plans to keep developing his overseas market for both events and performers. Many American musicians are keen to travel abroad, and a U.S. gig is still a dream for thousands of foreign musicians. Seeing globalization at work in the music business, Panay says that American bands no longer compete for an event just with another band down the street; now many might be competing for an event with a band from Berlin and another from Budapest. Sonicbids has also made deals with European export promotion offices, which view their musicians' performances abroad as a source of both revenue for the home country and good public relations.

Nor does Panay's vision stop with the music business. He has only begun to tap what he sees as another neglected market, one potentially far bigger than the market for musical gigs. Jugglers and magicians have already signed up as members of Sonicbids, and Panay has had inquiries from actors, supermodels, and freelance writers. He suspects that speakers might be interested, too, and a bridge to that multibillion-dollar market already exists; Sonicbids has done deals with colleges, which frequently need speakers for their events.

With all that he has going on, Panay knows he must stay flexible enough to adjust to unexpected demands. Already some end customers are looking to bypass existing middlemen, such as agents, and deal directly with Sonicbids. "I never dreamed that video-game companies would want anything to do with us," he told me, "but here they come." They are looking for bargains and simple deals from Sonicbids, he says, because "they don't want to pay $500,000 to license some big artist's music or deal with her record label or publisher." Nor could Panay have ever guessed that wineries would be lining up on his site to find performers for their wine tastings, but some vintners are doing just that.

The big question for Panay is this: Will he be able to build the trust that will let him create a truly massive community? And if he succeeds in doing that, will he be able to leverage his business into something even broader? Might there be a way to use his relationships with the many people and businesses that use his site to interest major national advertisers?

At one point in our conversation, I asked Panay what drove him as a businessperson and as a leader. He replied, "The chance to move the needle of business history just a bit, and in a positive direction. When I wake up in the morning, that's my passion."

A powerful and inspiring response, worthy of a person who has harvested a rich crop in a field that nearly everyone else saw as barren.

GET SMART

▶ *Connect the dots.* Opportunities lurk in neglected fields everywhere, especially in places where people take dysfunction as the expected way of life. Talent agents have been besieged for years by too many resumes, DVDs, and press kits from aspiring musicians, and musicians have been frustrated for just as long by their inability to get a hearing. It took Panay to see that the gap could be bridged and to find the right way to do it.

ρ **Think global**

Every business today—
no matter how small—can
be global. To succeed,
though, requires ambition,
understanding customers'
needs, solid partners, and
knowing how information
technology can be best used
to advantage.

It bears repeating that ideas like Panay's
musician matchmaking service are hiding
in plain sight around the world. It doesn't
take a business wizard or money to find
them—only a sharp eye for an unmet need
and a willingness to work hard to figure out
how best to fulfill that need. You can look
in your own industry for the same kind of
opportunity Panay discovered. Map out the
players—your customers, suppliers, business
partners, and even competitors. How do
products, services, information, and money
flow between these players, and where do
the breakdowns occur? Where are people
underserved? Where are there dysfunctions?
Then try to connect the dots in different
ways to bring value to all the players. Finding
the opportunities is part science and part art.
Panay has proved himself a artful fellow.

▶ *Think global.* The Internet allowed a business
based in Boston's South End to have a true
global reach. Sonicbids has one office, but
it is quickly becoming a global giant. That's
because Panay recognized at the outset
that the music industry has no borders. It's
not just that people in Iceland want to hear
American music, but bands from Iceland
want to play in Yonkers, New York, and
people in Yonkers want to hear music from
Turkey.

Panay had the advantage of growing up in Cyprus and the opportunity to develop international sensibilities. You can do almost the same, but you'll have to do more than just stroll down the street to see who your customers are. Get on a plane and cross an ocean or two to see how your product or service would be received. Some markets for products and services will remain "local," but global players will enter even those markets—think healthcare. Because of technology, your customers, business partners, and competitors are everywhere.

▶ *Scale quickly.* When Panay told me that he had 120,000 performers registered at Sonicbids, I was incredulous. But that's what it takes to capture this kind of market. Scale is important when you are building any kind of community-based business. People will go to the service that offers the most choice—assuming, of course, that the quality of your service is equal or better than that of your competitors'.

But achieving scale is not just about signing up people. Your service has to offer value to all participants. That's what keeps people in your game and active in your business. Promoters, musicians, and the eventual clients all get value from Sonicbids's services—and the value goes far beyond just enabling a search.

▶ *Keep checking your intuition.* When Panay introduced a new feature on Sonicbids, the feedback button, without checking it with his customers, he was looking for trouble—and he got it. As smart as he was about what his customers needed, he couldn't know how they would react—and neither does any manager or marketer.

Particularly in today's business climate, with its smarter, plugged-in consumers, you can't afford to take a chance with a major change. Check it out so that you can spot the pitfalls and profit thereby.

As Panay later demonstrated by choosing analytical managers who balanced out the weak spots in his own nature, an executive who tends to go with his gut in making decisions needs to have someone around who will say, "Hold on a second. Let me run the numbers."

▶ *Pay attention to service.* Many people who get caught up with a new business model or technology tend to give scant attention to the quality of their customer service. That's a serious error. People who run technology-based businesses are particularly susceptible to this error. They seem to think that technology itself will solve customer problems; think of those hated customer service centers with no service people and endless automated transfers. High-tech businesses still require lots of human interaction—and, as Panay points out, a little human touch can help define the character and feel of your business.

"YOU CAN'T EXPECT YOUR KNOWLEDGE OF YESTERDAY TO CARRY YOU THROUGH TOMORROW."

▶ *Don't stop thinking about tomorrow.* You might think Panay would relax a bit and rest on his laurels. After all, the growth rate of Sonicbids has been out of sight. He knows better. As he told me, he's a voracious reader, constantly searching for more information to add to his memory bank, constantly trying to upgrade himself. He has no problem admitting that he knows little about a certain matter before asking someone to explain it to him. He's not afraid—nor should he be—that being humble in that way will lessen his staff's admiration of his leadership. What's more, his plans for expansion and his visionary notion of how large his neglected field might be are both bold and sensible. "You can't expect your knowledge of yesterday to carry you through tomorrow," he commented at one point. That pretty much says it all.

QUESTIONS TO ASK YOURSELF

- ▶ Do you know where the breakdowns occur in your industry? Where customers have unfulfilled and bad experiences? Where money gets lost or left on the table?

- ▶ Can you turn these breakdowns and customer needs into a major business opportunity?

- ▶ Are you thinking in broad global terms about your markets? Do your products or services have to be altered to sell globally, or can you just reach out to global markets?

- ▶ Is your ambition large enough? Can you scale your business proposition easily? How large does your business have to be to grow and sustain itself?

- ▶ Is there value for all those you must engage in your business model? How can you deliver enough value to keep people coming to your business?

▶ Do you have people or processes to check on your own intuitive calls, to catch a stumble or to fix a break? Are you prepared to be vulnerable and have people tell you that you are wrong?

▶ Have you invested enough in the service component of your work? Are you too dependant on technology to self-fix customer problems?

▶ How will your customers experience the character and feel of your business?

▶ What will tomorrow bring, in both opportunity and challenge? How will you respond?

IT WAS A DAZZLING SPRING MORNING IN MINNESOTA, BUT JODI WEST COULD BARELY SEE IT. SHE AWOKE WITH A RED, PAINFUL, AND WATERING RIGHT EYE. BEFORE SHE COULD SEEK HELP, THE SYMPTOMS HAD INVADED HER LEFT EYE. UNFORTUNATELY, IT WAS SATURDAY AND, NO SURPRISE, HER DOCTOR WAS ALLERGIC TO WEEKEND OFFICE HOURS. WEST COULD TAKE HERSELF TO A HOSPITAL EMERGENCY ROOM, BUT THIS WAS NO DAY FOR CAMPING OUT IN AN OVERCROWDED AND SLOW-MOVING ER. HER SEVEN-YEAR-OLD DAUGHTER WAS SCHEDULED TO DANCE IN TWO RECITALS. WEST WAS ALREADY OVERDUE TO BE DRIVING HER THERE.

CHAPTER 3

Compete by Thinking outside the Bubble: MinuteClinic Delivers Healthcare Retail

This is no sad story, though—quite the opposite. West simply zipped off to a nearby Target store. At a colorful kiosk close to the pharmacy section, a cheerful nurse practitioner examined her and confirmed her suspicion ("Yes, it's an infection") and wrote a prescription. West was back on the road in 20 minutes with a bill for $44.

The kiosk was an outpost of MinuteClinic, a classic example of a company whose founders recognized a significant unmet consumer need and seized the opportunity by borrowing an idea from a seemingly unrelated industry. What began as a notion for a few partners in Minneapolis eight years ago has blossomed into a coast-to-coast operation serving more than 500,000 customers a year. And when CVS Caremark Corporation bought the company in 2007, the all-cash payoff for the founders was $170 million.

ρ **Emergency room**

Minute Clinic gives patients—and insurance companies—an alternative to the emergency room. Its business model challenges how healthcare is delivered and is just the kind of breakthrough that the industry needs.

Why do some people easily spot opportunities where others see only obstacles, if they see anything? The answer begins with the human penchant for living in a bubble—an airtight cocoon of assumptions, beliefs, or worldviews.

WHY DO SOME PEOPLE EASILY SPOT OPPORTUNITIES WHERE OTHERS SEE ONLY OBSTACLES, IF THEY SEE ANYTHING? THE ANSWER BEGINS WITH THE HUMAN PENCHANT FOR LIVING IN A BUBBLE—AN AIRTIGHT COCOON OF ASSUMPTIONS, BELIEFS, OR WORLDVIEWS.

The bubble mentality shows itself in a runaway bull market, for example, when speculators who should be thinking about sharply escalating risks are blinded by greed. Convinced that soaring prices will keep going up indefinitely, they keep on buying. And then one day they are blind sided when the bubble bursts.

The good thing about business bubbles, however, is that they invite inventive minds to stick pins in them. MinuteClinic's founders were bubble bursters, creative guerrillas who thrive on outsmarting complacent companies in industries that run on tired ideas. Bubble bursters come in all cultural shapes and financial sizes, but they share one indispensable trait: They see what others can't, and they act on it by applying solid practices that everyone else agrees are irrelevant to their industry or company.

Admittedly, it's a challenge to peer outside the bubble, see problems waiting to be solved, and find solutions in other companies or industries that no one else has thought to apply to your field. But it's not impossible. The initial prescription is simple: Open yourself to seeing the bigger picture so you can assess what others are doing that will actually work in your industry and your company.

OPEN YOURSELF TO SEEING THE BIGGER PICTURE SO YOU CAN ASSESS WHAT OTHERS ARE DOING THAT WILL ACTUALLY WORK IN YOUR INDUSTRY AND YOUR COMPANY.

The MinuteClinic story is a fascinating tale in its own right, but it also offers general insights along with specific details of how some people saw what others could not. It is a lesson in outsmarting competitors by trying ideas that they think have nothing to do with their industry. Let's wheel out our x-ray machine and take a closer look.

MEDICINE (MOSTLY) WITHOUT DOCTORS

The kiosk West visited in the Minneapolis Target was built on this premise: Many common ailments do not require treatment by a physician or a hospital emergency room, and can be safely, inexpensively, and rapidly handled by a well-trained nurse practitioner. Stated that way, it sounds more like common sense than a revolutionary idea; after all, it's no different from Jiffy Lube's insight that you don't need a fully trained mechanic to change the oil in your car. But until MinuteClinic's founders came along, no one in the healthcare field would have dreamed that they could learn anything from the grubby business of auto maintenance. And in practice, MinuteClinic's road from insight to reality was full of rough spots and barriers.

Here's how MinuteClinic works: The company's kiosks are open seven days a week for a total of at least 72 hours. The kiosks clearly post the ailments that can be treated there, along with the fees. Some two dozen medical issues, ranging from allergies and athlete's foot to sinus infections and suture removal, are treated at prices that seldom exceed $59 a visit, and insurance covers most of that. Children younger than 18 months are not accepted as patients because diagnosis is often difficult in the very young.

Generally, one nurse practitioner staffs each kiosk, and she or he has both a four-year bachelor's degree and a two-year master's degree in nursing, plus a license to prescribe drugs. But only verifiable, quickly identifiable illnesses are treated. The company has strict protocols and screening procedures, backed by sophisticated software, to confirm a diagnosis and rule out really serious conditions. For example, the software directs that a child with an inflamed ear and a fever of more than 101.5° Fahrenheit be referred immediately to a doctor. Each kiosk also has a physician on call if the nurse has any doubts or concerns, and a report on each visit is faxed to a patient's primary caregiver.

Most visitors to MinuteClinic are treated within 10 to 15 minutes. But if several people arrive at the same time and stretch the wait beyond 5 minutes, the company has a smart and simple solution: Patients receive pagers that enable them to shop in the surrounding store until they're buzzed.

The idea for MinuteClinic grew out of a family emergency one winter weekend in 1999, when entrepreneur Rick Krieger's son turned up with a very sore throat. Knowing the boy needed a test to rule out strep throat, Krieger drove him to an emergency care center in Minneapolis. After a two-hour wait, their time came. The test proved negative.

At the time, Krieger and some friends, including a physician and a registered nurse, were thinking about setting up a web site for doctors. Learning that WebMD was already up and running, they cast about for another idea. Krieger mentioned the experience with his son. Why, he wondered, wasn't there a quick and convenient way to get treatment for simple medical problems? The group filled the void the following year with a company initially called QuickMedx (the MinuteClinic name came later). They installed their first healthcare kiosks in Cub Foods stores around the Minneapolis–St. Paul area.

Early interest was lackluster. The kiosks drew an average of 8 to 12 patients per day, hardly enough to cover costs. Then a local union leader got on board. His members were being charged anywhere from $70 to $150 per doctor or clinic visit, 80 percent of which the union reimbursed. It was an easy decision for the union to cover 100 percent of the mini-clinics' flat fee, which was then $35: If a member went to QuickMedx and avoided a

$100 doctor's bill, the union would save $45. Mining that lode, QuickMedx went on to recruit associations of meat packers, auto dealers, electricians, and bakery drivers.

At first, the company rejected patients' medical insurance, hoping to avoid the deluge of paperwork, delayed payments, and all the other frustrations of what Krieger called "the whole insurance game." But customer resistance soon reversed that decision, and shortly afterward, Blue Cross and Blue Shield of Minnesota, which insures fully one-third of all covered Minnesotans, decided that it, too, could save money by reimbursing its clients for virtually all their QuickMedx bills. As part of the deal, the big insurer promised there would be no payment delays or extra paperwork for QuickMedx.

But from the start, the clinics met opposition from the medical establishment. Doctors questioned the quality of care and complained that the nurse practitioners didn't have access to patients' comprehensive medical records—necessary, the physicians claimed, for safe treatment. "I worry about bringing medical care to the discount store," the president of the Minnesota Medical Association intoned. "What if the patient has a bad reaction to a shot or is sicker than the nurse practitioner realizes? You could call 911 from Cub Foods, but I don't regard that as the right kind of approach."

With such formidable critics, QuickMedx was looking rather sickly itself two years after start-up. The clinics had treated only 49,000 patients, the company's losses surpassed $2.8 million, and new capital was scarce. Initially backed by 14 local investors, QuickMedx held little appeal for venture capitalists in the medical field, whose interest centered on high-tech gadgets, and retail investors were scared away by the medical controversy. Finally, Bain Capital Ventures stepped up to take a 28 percent stake in the company. Soon after, the founders left and major changes were made.

Linda Hall Whitman, a former Honeywell Corporation executive, took over as CEO, and Dr. Glen Nelson, a surgeon who had been vice chairman of Medtronic, became board chairman. In short order, the company raised prices, reeled in $4 million in new capital, and upgraded the clinics' software to include guidelines on the latest best practices in diagnosis and treatment, along with a drug-interaction database. QuickMedx also doubled the number of ailments treated and increased its menu of services. For example, in the winter of 2004, when influenza vaccine was in short supply nationwide, the company began offering a nasal swab test for the flu and followed up on positive results with a prescription.

The MinuteClinic name came about after Whitman and Nelson learned that someone outside the state had trademarked the QuickMedx name. Because they were planning to expand the company beyond Minnesota, they would have to change the name—and they did. But out-of-state expansion was put on hold as the team concentrated on growth in Minnesota. Additional kiosks were placed in Target stores and in the headquarters of several companies, including Best Buy and Guidant. The better value provided by MinuteClinic prompted some employers to offer reduced co-pays for employees who used the clinics. One company, St. Jude Medical, a medical device maker in St. Paul, says MinuteClinic saved 1,700 of its workers a total of $20,000 a year in health costs.

Whitman stepped down as chief executive in 2005 and was
succeeded by Michael C. Howe, a veteran marketer at Procter &
Gamble and Helene Curtis. Howe, whose resume also includes
four years as CEO of fast-food purveyor Arby's, told me about
his hiring: "In the first interview on May 6, I said, 'Guys, I love
the concept, I love it. But you made a mistake—I'm not a
healthcare guy.'" That was just fine with those doing the hiring,
and less than a month later, Howe was in the driver's seat. As
it turned out, bringing a superb marketer to retail healthcare
was just what the doctor should have ordered. The bubble
that so often makes medical providers oblivious to customers'
needs was about to meet a sharp pin, much to the benefit of
MinuteClinic's financial health.

When Howe arrived, Nelson described his job as building the
systems, processes, and structure that would be essential if
MinuteClinic was to have a national footprint. Two years later,
the company had gone from 19 clinics in two markets to 83
clinics in 10 states, and it received a marriage proposal from
CVS Caremark, the largest retail pharmacy in the United States.
Now, as part of the CVS empire, which counted more than
6,000 retail and specialty stores in 43 states and the District
of Columbia in 2007, MinuteClinic's bright little kiosks will be
visible nearly everywhere.

Before examining how Howe worked his magic, let's step back
to look at the broader picture, including the foundation his
predecessors laid. The company's founders had the vision
to think outside the bubble; they dove in to grab an obvious
opportunity that others couldn't see by applying retailing
practices to healthcare. It also took considerable courage on the

part of Krieger and his associates to create a retail healthcare delivery system in the face of the medical establishment.

When Howe came along, he finished bursting the healthcare bubble by shifting MinuteClinic's focus. Whereas everyone else in healthcare was concentrating on solving the problems of diagnosis and treatment, he said MinuteClinic "focused on changing how healthcare is delivered." The shift was at once simple and profound.

The profundity relates to the fact that healthcare is a very tough industry to change. Physicians call the shots not just within their own practices, but in hospitals and clinics as well. State laws, largely dictated by physicians, control who can provide healthcare. What's more, doctors have an emotional hold on all of us. We've been raised to accept gratefully whatever a physician serves up. Howe likens a doctor to the Wizard of Oz—no one dares to look behind the curtain. When we get our cars fixed, we go to the garage when it's convenient for us, we ask what's wrong, and we question, maybe even haggle over, the price. But as Howe pointed out, "With a doctor, you take the first appointment, you wait in the office forever without complaint, you accept what the doctor says without challenge, and you never talk about price."

What MinuteClinic saw that others either didn't see or simply ignored were the fault lines in the system. The healthcare challenge in America today is enormous, and patients might be running out of both patience and the money needed to pay soaring fees. The old doctor-driven mode of delivering healthcare is under siege. Indeed, more people use the Internet to make themselves smarter about their physical problems. They are also asking physicians to explain diagnoses and treatments with more candor and clarity. What might come as a surprise to some is that more than a few doctors seem happy, even relieved, to oblige.

At the same time, health insurance costs have skyrocketed while eligibility declines, leaving scores of millions of Americans uninsured. In many parts of the country, patients—even those in great pain—must spend hours waiting for care in hospital emergency rooms. It's no exaggeration to say that you risk your life if you get sick or injured at night or on a weekend.

Howe's strategy was shrewd and, in hindsight, obvious: MinuteClinic would address parts of all these dysfunctions by biting off the easiest, least complex chunk of the healthcare market. What I learned from my conversations with Howe is that the company's success actually derives from a critical understanding of both medical and retail value, a lively blend that Nelson and Howe bring to the table. They have taken a crucial step toward making healthcare standardized, convenient, and affordable. That's a goal that might never be fully attainable—open-heart surgery and cancer care, for instance, aren't ever likely to be off-the-shelf offerings. But there's no reason why the MinuteClinic model couldn't be applied, with precautions and modifications, to a whole range of ailments and procedures that have become standard practice in healthcare.

Nelson, who oversees the constant upgrading of the company's healthcare delivery, has also built bridges to the medical community, reassuring his peers that MinuteClinic has high standards of care and strong safeguards to prevent mistakes. He has even developed partnerships with other, more traditional caregivers, including a few hospitals that have invited MinuteClinic to set up kiosks in their facilities. For these enlightened hospitals, it's a boon to have nurse practitioners take over simple chores that would otherwise tie up doctors and add to their long lines of "emergency" patients. These days, MinuteClinic is even getting patients referred to its kiosks by overworked doctors and hospital emergency rooms.

As for Howe's contribution from the retail side, he describes his input as "teaching the nurse practitioners to be service oriented and patient centric." For example, in handling complaints (something with which healthcare providers typically have little experience), "we're teaching people not only how to remediate the complaint," he says, "but to embrace it as a learning experience." He points out that although a complaint can destroy a career in the healthcare field, a complaint in retail can be beneficial because it tells people on the front line what the customer wants. It provides a chance to improve service. (Of course, the same would be true for healthcare if complaints were handled properly.)

The next logical step, Howe told me, was to instill greater sensitivity in the nurse practitioners so they could head off complaints before they erupted into full-blown problems. For example, Howe urges them to pick up on customers' body language, including the folded arms and constant checking of watches that signal impatience. Or if a woman with two screaming children is third on the waiting list, he suggests that the nurse ask those ahead if they would mind letting her be seen first.

As for marketing the business, Howe sums up his mission in these words: "Reach and teach." The company needs to "emotionally reach consumers" to communicate the value of MinuteClinic, he says, and "teach them what it is and isn't, and how best to use it."

AS FOR MARKETING THE BUSINESS, HOWE SUMS UP HIS MISSION IN THESE WORDS: "REACH AND TEACH." THE COMPANY NEEDS TO "EMOTIONALLY REACH CONSUMERS" TO COMMUNICATE THE VALUE OF MINUTECLINIC, HE SAYS, AND "TEACH THEM WHAT IT IS AND ISN'T, AND HOW BEST TO USE IT."

The biggest challenge Howe and his company face is the regulatory minefield laid down by state medical lobbyists trying to defend their turf. The rules go back to the nineteenth century, are immensely complicated, and vary from state to state. In most states, they add up to a monopoly on medical care and represent old assumptions about where knowledge and skills reside, which boil down to this: "Only a business run by physicians can treat you." But state by state, MinuteClinic is chipping away at the regulations and successfully opening new clinics. Howe is optimistic. He thinks reform is inevitable, and history would seem to support that view. Not surprisingly, Howe is also confident that MinuteClinic will soon be a household name.

GET SMART

▶ *Widen your lens.* By viewing the healthcare industry in a retail context, the founders of MinuteClinic were able to identify an anomaly: Many simple complaints that didn't need a doctor's attention were nonetheless being treated, elaborately and expensively, in physicians' offices and hospital emergency rooms. Retailing offered an obvious alternative: Just as Jiffy Lube and Midas Muffler perform small repairs and services without fully trained mechanics, mini-clinics could give shots, treat sore throats, and prescribe flu medicine without a doctor on the premises. The service could be quick, convenient, and inexpensive.

Why did no one else see this opportunity? Bubble thinking is common in large medical centers, and it is absolutely rampant in research and teaching facilities. The irony is that one would imagine very smart people to be more capable, not less, when it comes to understanding and responding to the needs of their customer-patients. But my experience with the healthcare industry has shown just the opposite: With the exception of perhaps the Mayo Clinic, usually the better the clinical care is, the worse the customer service is.

Patients typically endure long waits, fill out multiple and redundant forms and are forced to navigate a complex and confounding set of systems and processes without guidance. And if they ask for help, they often receive a frosty response. The problem is that clinicians are focused on providing good medicine, not great service.

Most patients, myself included, have been willing to trade amenities such as shorter wait times and simplified paperwork for the best clinical care. But we don't have to, and that points to another opportunity for healthcare providers. Even at the high end of the industry, outside the MinuteClinic model, great care and satisfactory customer service are not mutually exclusive. Medical personnel and hospital administrators merely need to take their cue from the retailing and hospitality industries, where streamlined check-in procedures and quick response to customer requests are standard operating procedure.

▶ *Make friends.* Your number one goal, of course, is to outsmart your competitors. But after you've done that, it's time to think about cooling things down. No one wins in an industry war. MinuteClinic has gone to great pains to reach out to physicians and hospitals to explain its operations and earn their trust. As Howe told me, "Our message is that we want to be part of the solution, a partner, not a head-to-head competitor."

Conflict resolution frees up a lot of energy and resources that can be devoted to the business. It also provides an opportunity to sell your services to your one-time rivals. That's what MinuteClinic has done, reaping thousands of referrals from overworked full-service clinics and hospital emergency rooms.

You will make friends more easily if you offer services that not only benefit your customers and your company, but also address the ills of your entire industry. People in an industry such as healthcare, with its many moving parts and multiple players, can be brought more easily to a shared table if there is something in it for everyone. I don't know of a single patient, employer, bill payer, hospital administrator, insurance company, nurse, or physician who doesn't want a more efficient healthcare system. A business such as MinuteClinic is offering a new model from which an entire industry can learn and benefit. Ask yourself if your business model can lead your industry to needed change.

YOU WILL MAKE FRIENDS MORE EASILY IF YOU OFFER SERVICES THAT NOT ONLY BENEFIT YOUR CUSTOMERS AND YOUR COMPANY, BUT ALSO ADDRESS THE ILLS OF YOUR ENTIRE INDUSTRY.

▶ *Execute on the change.* Identifying a problem and finding an out-of-context business practice to emulate is only the first step. Next comes the careful implementation of your idea. For MinuteClinic, execution meant building a company that could deliver both high-quality healthcare and a high standard of service, and changes had to be made in people, processes, and technology to get the job done.

Sometimes people are able to adjust to the life a new business model dictates, and sometimes staffing changes are necessary. In filling its nurse practitioner slots, MinuteClinic paid a good deal of attention to personalities and skills. It sought people who were both clinically competent and well attuned to customer sensibilities. The company strictly enforced its rules on what could and couldn't be treated, and it backed up its standard diagnostic and treatment procedures with the latest technology.

As you progress through this book, you will find that nearly all the companies cited have fine-tuned their people, processes, and technology to meld them into a smoothly operating machine that delivers more value to the customer. And similar to a piece of precision-made machinery, any breakdown in the business sets off alarms.

▶ *Redefine the culture.* You can't take anything for granted when you create a bubble-bursting business model. You need to establish a culture that will support what you're trying to achieve. Howe recognized that nurse practitioners are, by nature, caring, empathetic individuals, but they are not in the retail business (unless they already work for MinuteClinic). His understanding of the distinction led him to create a customer-centric culture that was exemplified by his program to teach MinuteClinic nurses to welcome complaints as a way of improving their service.

AND IF YOU DON'T TRUST YOUR PEOPLE TO ADAPT, YOU HAVE THE WRONG PEOPLE IN PLACE. I STRONGLY BELIEVE THAT YOU CHANGE HOW PEOPLE THINK BY CHANGING WHAT THEY DO.

People need to learn quickly how to behave as the new business model demands. You might lecture them about the required behavior change or take them on an adventure in the woods and make them scale walls and climb ropes (a popular practice these days). But in my experience, lectures and rope-climbing exercises are too far removed from the real work people do to effect sustainable change. To change the culture in your business, get people off the ropes and on the firm ground of doing real work inside your new business model as quickly as possible. And if you don't trust your people to adapt, you have the wrong people in place. I strongly believe that you change how people think by changing what they do.

QUESTIONS TO ASK YOURSELF

▶ Are you looking beyond your industry to discern how to deliver more value to your customers?

▶ Which customer needs are going unmet within your own industry? Can you find a similar problem that has been solved in another field? Could that model be modified to work for you?

▶ Have you made a hard assessment of how your customers rate the performance of your company and industry?

▶ Can you change your business model in ways that will point the entire industry toward better performance?

▶ Would your customers and company benefit from collaboration with other companies, even your competitors?

- ▶ What changes to people, processes, and technology would be required if you changed your business model?

- ▶ What cultural and behavioral changes would you need to make within your company?

- ▶ Would your people be able to adapt?

WHEN THE RECRUITER CALLED THAT WINTER OF 2004, MICHAEL GOLDEN WAS CONTENTEDLY PRESIDING OVER THE KOHLER COMPANY'S CABINETRY DIVISION. NOT LOOKING FOR A NEW POST, HE THOUGHT THE CALL WAS A WASTE OF TIME. BUT WHEN HE LEARNED THAT THE WHOLE BOARD OF AN UNNAMED PUBLIC COMPANY WAS WAITING TO INTERVIEW HIM, HE COULDN'T RESIST.

CHAPTER 4

COMPETE BY USING ALL YOU KNOW: BASICS ARE BLAZING AT SMITH & WESSON

The company, it turned out, was Smith & Wesson (S&W), the 150-year-old firearms manufacturer, and it was in dire straits. Its chairman had been exposed as a convicted felon, federal agents were investigating accounting irregularities, a countrywide boycott had driven down sales, and the stock price had plummeted to $1 a share. The company clearly needed rescuing, and the board decided Golden was the right person for the job. He was invited to become president and chief executive.

On the face of it, this was not a match made in heaven. Golden had never been a CEO, and he knew nothing about the arms industry. The company's owners and managers had always been engineers and manufacturers, and he was mostly a marketer. He had never fired a gun and didn't even know the difference between

ρ **Smith & Wesson headquarters**

When I walked the factory floor of Smith & Wesson's plant in Western Massachusetts, the energy and commitment of its people were palpable. It was evident that every employee is striving to make the business ever more efficient and contributing to the revival of the corporation.

ρ **Smith & Wesson revolver**

Michael Golden didn't put a gun to his organization's collective head, but he did demand that his managers and employees return to business fundamentals.

an automatic pistol and a revolver. Yet the
more he learned about the organization,
the more he realized that his years at Kohler
and earlier stints at Stanley Works and Black
& Decker had given him the skills Smith &
Wesson desperately needed. As Golden told
me years later, "I just seemed to know how to
do this."

Smith & Wesson held undeniable appeal as
an American legend. It had armed thousands
of Civil War combatants, Western settlers,
and U.S. cavalrymen. Armies, navies, and
police agencies around the world favored
S&W's 1899-vintage Model 10 revolver. Clint
Eastwood brandished its .44 Magnum in the
Dirty Harry movies. Golden's children were
fascinated by the offer. When his two oldest
twenty-somethings heard about it, he recalls,
"They looked at me and said, 'Dad, you're
going to become a bad-ass.'"

© CinemaPhotos/CORBIS.

Golden took the job. But when he was assured on his first day that Smith & Wesson "kind of runs itself," he thought he knew where the trouble had started. "No company runs itself," he told me. "Here was this organization with a world-class brand and loyal, dedicated employees, and there was no leadership pulling it all together, nobody who really knew what was going on."

When we talked, Golden had been running S&W for less than three years, but he had already achieved extraordinary results. The company's revenues had soared from $100 million for the fiscal year ending in April 2003 to $237 million for the fiscal year ending in April 2007. From its nadir of $1 a share, the stock had soared to about $23. Russ Thurman, editor of *Shooting* magazine, said it all: "No company in modern history has come back from the dead like Smith & Wesson. In the dark days, you'd go to a trade show and there would be an invisible cone of silence around the Smith & Wesson booth. Now you have to get into a fist fight to get close to their displays."

How did Golden bring about the turnaround? By leveraging everything he'd learned from more than two decades in business, proving once again that accumulated wisdom can be a powerful weapon in the fight to outsmart your competitors. In one way or another, all the strategies he employed at S&W, the new processes he put in place, the thinking that led to an acquisition, and the leap into new markets were the outgrowth of events encountered and actions taken in his previous corporate life. His achievement shows how using everything you know can help you outsmart your rivals.

◠ **Horace Smith and Daniel Wesson**

The company's founders exemplified the persistence required to build a successful—and fabled — company. Golden saw value in what they created, and he set about to leverage the company's history as part of his turnaround strategy.

It might sound obvious to apply what you already know to real-life challenges, but it takes discipline. So often we forget history—even when we are part of the story—and we all know that history repeats itself. We tend to compartmentalize our knowledge, neglecting to apply a lesson we've learned to a problem that comes up in another context. It then takes hard concentration and imagination to dredge up past cases and apply them to the present. Golden forgot nothing and used everything.

WE TEND TO COMPARTMENTALIZE OUR KNOWLEDGE, NEGLECTING TO APPLY A LESSON WE'VE LEARNED TO A PROBLEM THAT COMES UP IN ANOTHER CONTEXT.

Unlike most of the companies featured in this book, Smith & Wesson itself was both venerable and storied—and one of

PHOTO COURTESY OF BIGCOUNTRY.
WWW.BIGCOUNTRY.DE.

PHOTO COURTESY OF BIGCOUNTRY.
WWW.BIGCOUNTRY.DE.

its problems was that it had forgotten or simply ignored the lessons of its own history. Back in 1854, Horace Smith and Daniel B. Wesson first set up shop in Norwich, Connecticut. They had a new idea: the Volcanic, a lever-action pistol using self-contained cartridges. But they were better producers than promoters. Sales faltered and they were forced to sell out to a shirt maker, Oliver Winchester, who eventually used their lever-action design in producing his legendary Winchester repeating rifle.

Undiscouraged, Smith and Wesson formed their eponymous company in 1856. They created the first successful revolver with a self-contained cartridge. And this time, helped by Civil War demand, they prospered. By 1870, they had sold 1,000 of the guns to the U.S. Cavalry.

The next century saw far more ups than downs for the company, and by the 1970s, S&W was the top gun in the sidearm market, which includes hunters, sport shooters, and the military. It also armed 98 percent of America's policemen. But then foreign arms makers with breakthrough designs crept through Customs, and S&W was too complacent to see its peril. In the 1980s, Austria's Glock began pitching its lightweight polymer pistol to American police departments. S&W scoffed, confident that no officer would want to carry a plastic weapon. Within a few years, Glock had stolen virtually the entire police market, cutting S&W's share from 98 percent to single digits. In 1987, Tomkins of London purchased the struggling S&W for only $112 million.

In 2000, trying to escape further losses, Smith & Wesson got itself dropped from state and federal lawsuits brought against the gun industry by agreeing to a variety of gun-safety measures, including background checks on gun buyers. A furious National Rifle Association orchestrated the reprisal: Gun owners mounted a boycott, cutting even deeper into S&W's sales. When Tomkins offloaded S&W to an American investment group in 2001, the fire-sale price was a mere $15 million. After three more years of floundering, the investment group turned to Golden.

Applying experience to solve problems starts with learning everything you can about the problem. Golden had been at S&W's headquarters in Springfield, Massachusetts, for less than a week when he asked what he thought was a basic question: "How are we doing?" The answer that slowly emerged, he says, vindicated his hunch that the basic problem at S&W might be that it was running itself. "Nobody knew. The manufacturing guys were just making stuff, whether we needed it or not. The sales guys had no target—they didn't know whether we needed $10 million or $20 million that month. No one was talking to anyone."

That began to change the very next morning at 8:30, when Golden called to order the first of what would become daily meetings with vice presidents and their top aides in charge of sales, operations, and other major areas. It was Management 101, but a revelation for S&W's people. The sessions revolved around exchanging information: The salespeople would report on the orders received the day before, the manufacturing people on the number of products turned out, and so on. In each case, the reality was compared to a target number. If a discrepancy existed, explanations were expected, and whoever fell short had to submit a plan for getting back on track.

Brand management was a skill Golden had picked up at Kohler, and he soon began to do extensive research to learn everything he could about the Smith & Wesson brand. He found that its awareness level was 87 percent, an amazing figure for a company with just $100 million in sales. And it didn't matter whether the interviewees liked guns, whether they were male or female, or whether they lived on the East or West Coast. Their reaction to S&W was extremely positive. The brand radiated Americana—the Civil War, the Wild West, Clint Eastwood.

Next Golden and his company set out to learn how their customers felt about the brand. S&W asked 3,500 hunters, shooters, and sports enthusiasts some bread-and-butter questions. If they were going to buy a revolver, what brand would they buy? What brand of automatic pistol? S&W scored at the top in both categories, to no one's surprise. Then they were asked what brand of shotgun they would buy. The company came in third—even though it didn't manufacture shotguns or any other long guns. The same thing happened when the subjects were asked about bolt-action hunting rifles, ammunition, and even home security systems, all markets that Smith & Wesson had no presence in. The company still ranked near the top in preferences.

"Coming in, I thought the brand had a lot of legs," Golden recalls. "The research told us just how much power it had."

The strategy of his predecessors had been to dominate a niche market, focusing entirely on handguns in the United States. Golden had much grander goals. To begin, he wanted to expand the handgun business by a quantum leap. Then he planned to diversify into other markets where the brand had such clear potential magic. Overall, he wanted to push the brand to ever-greater heights of recognition and approval so that it would support and advance all the company's projects.

The sales side of the company was divided into four channels—sporting goods, the federal government (including the military), state and municipal police, and foreign governments. With the exception of a few large retailers, independent dealers across the country rule the market for sport guns used in hunting and target shooting. S&W had its own salespeople for the eastern half of the country and relied on independent agents for the western half. These representatives sold a variety of sports products, including fishing tackle and firearms, but their results did not impress Golden.

Again he set out to learn the facts. He commissioned research that showed that the company's own sales staff, with no special training, sold three times more than the reps. Golden wasn't surprised. He had learned long ago that "you get what you pay for." So he fired the independent agents and hired new salesmen to take over the western territory.

At nearly every turn, Golden applied lessons learned at previous jobs. To boost sales, for example, he fell back on what he'd learned about demand creation when he helped launch the DeWalt power-tool division of Black & Decker. "We didn't spend the company's money on TV commercials," he told me. "We did hand-to-hand combat on the retail level."

S&W created an extensive training program for its own salespeople, both the veterans and those hired to pick up the slack left by the fired reps. They were taught how to train the dealers in merchandising their products, and how to organize special events at their area stores or shooting ranges so that people could have the experience of handling and firing the weapons.

The results were so counterintuitive that they make Golden laugh to this day. In the first quarter of 2004, after firing half of the company's salespeople and with their replacements just getting their feet wet, sales rose 8 percent from the previous year's level. During the next three quarters, sales jumped by 32, 37, and 52 percent, respectively.

Despite the company's name recognition and stellar reputation, the U.S. government has been a hard sell for S&W in recent years. During his get-acquainted tour of the company, Golden was amazed to find that the American armed forces were not using a single handgun manufactured by an American company—and the 100,000 pistols the United States was giving to the Iraqi military police had been bought from Austria's Glock. But the reasons became clear when Golden discovered another aspect of S&W's self-running era: Despite the fact that one of the company's four sales tracks was supposed to be the federal government, no one was responsible for government sales. Oh, and by the way, S&W had no lobbying representation in Washington.

ρ **The Pentagon**
By focusing on the federal
government market, Smith
& Wesson was able to regain
its position as a premier
provider of small arms to the
U.S. Defense Department.

In no time, Golden signed up a lobbying firm and hired an ex-Marine international shooting champion to ride herd on government sales. Golden himself started making regular trips to the capital, "talking our company," as he puts it, with influential members of Congress and the administration. The campaign has already paid off. S&W won all four of the contracts the American government put out to provide handguns for Afghanistan's military police, a $20 million piece of business.

Because S&W's old police revolver basically dated to 1899, the need to develop a new weapon to woo the law enforcement community was obvious. To accomplish this, says Golden, "We took another page from a company I worked for." As a product manager at Black & Decker, he had gone out on job sites to find out what his potential customers wanted in the way of tools.

Harold Flecknoe/Corbis Royalty Free

Now he dispatched his engineers and designers, along with his salespeople, to talk with state and city police officers about what they wanted in a pistol. The result is the sleek, powerful M&P 45 (Military and Police .45 caliber). Introduced in January 2006, the automatic pistol sports a reinforced polymer chassis, finally catching up with Glock.

The police market is a tough one to crack. The United States has 17,000 police departments, each of which conducts its own test and evaluation (T&E) studies before signing a contract. Some T&Es last as long as a year. Each department has different standards, depending on the preferences of the officers in charge. But the M&P 45 is clearly competitive. At this writing, it has won 80 percent of the tests it has entered.

The M&P 45 was also designed to fit the specifications for a new handgun for the U.S. armed forces, and S&W is pushing hard to

ρ **Public safety market**

Smith & Wesson had lost its leadership position in most markets, but it was able to leverage its still widely regarded brand to not only regain but surpass its previous business glory.

sell it to the Pentagon. At around $500 million, the contract will be the largest single pistol deal in history. "We think we'll be very competitive," Golden says.

Selling to foreign governments has been another challenge for S&W. Soon after 9/11, Congress passed a law requiring its approval for the sale of any U.S. firearms abroad when the order exceeds $1 million. Approval can easily take six months or more, putting a big crimp in the gun industry's foreign sales. Even so, S&W has achieved double-digit growth in that market as well.

In building his sales force, Golden faced a familiar choice. Should it be a single unit selling to all markets, or different units tailored to different markets? Once again, he drew on his past experience. "At Black & Decker, we went back and forth on whether to have a single sales group or have a split between consumer and professional sales groups," he told me. "We had the same question on whether the same people should sell both power tools and power accessories." In the end, as at Black & Decker, he decided that the two categories of S&W customers were too different to be well served by the same sales reps. He kept the sales groups separate.

When the handgun business was reorganized to his satisfaction, Golden embarked on his campaign to extend and leverage the S&W brand. His target: the long-gun market for rifles and shotguns, which, at $1 billion a year, was almost 60 percent larger than the market for handguns. His initial move, early in 2006, was a big event in the gun world. S&W introduced the first long gun in its 150-year history: a tactical rifle designed for both sporting shooters and military and police personnel, and made to S&W's specifications by an outside manufacturer.

With no more promotion than a press release, orders for the rifle poured in. "We were backlogged from day one," Golden remembers. Consumers snatched up the guns mainly for target shooting, and police departments were looking to replace their old pump shotguns with something more accurate at longer distances. In short order, S&W had 10 percent of the market, affirming Golden's confidence in the power of the brand.

In November 2006, another S&W press release announced the introduction of two new lines of lightweight, self-loading shotguns. Golden had lined up a supplier in Turkey to build a new factory and make the weapons. And along with the weapons, the company introduced a lifetime warranty program, the first of its kind in the firearms business.

ρ **Smith & Wesson rifle**
When Golden and his team discovered that the company had high consumer recognition in rifles—even though it had never actually made one—he entered the long gun business.

ρ **Hunters**

Golden was not a hunter—he had never even shot a gun before. But with a hunter's keen eye, he saw what his customers wanted and, with clear aim, hit his delivery targets.

The new year brought yet another diversification move. In January 2007, Golden announced the purchase of Thompson/Center Arms, a $65 million gun maker in Rochester, New Hampshire, with a 40-year history of good management and steady profits. Best of all, its line of hunting rifles meshed well with Golden's plans to invade that market. S&W, whose short-barrel handguns are acclaimed, was seeking additional know-how to produce superior long guns. Thompson provided that with its well-regarded, high-quality barrels.

Just three months later, S&W began marketing its own premium hunting rifle, with a Thompson/Center barrel and seven user-friendly patented features, including an adjustable trigger. The weapon was the first innovative bolt-action rifle in the United States in 25 years, and it was an instant hit in the hunting world.

Golden's expansion campaign is by no means over. He's looking into businesses such as home security and law-enforcement products such as body armor. But he's in no rush. Given all its new products, S&W is now fully engaged and free from any Wall Street pressure to show even more growth.

The U.S. firearms industry is not known for investing in new plants and equipment, but Golden—again drawing on lessons learned in his previous assignments—has so far put $40 million into innovative efficiencies at S&W's headquarters factory. That's more than all other U.S. gun makers combined have invested. The payoff has been a 7 percent jump in gross margin.

When Golden was at Stanley Works, he worked for John Trani, a member of Jack Welch's team at General Electric who absorbed that titan's penchant for cost containment. Golden practiced that lesson at S&W, introducing lean manufacturing techniques and supply-chain management to reduce expenses and raise productivity. The company has also introduced these practices at Thompson/Center, where long-gun barrel production has increased by 26 percent since the acquisition. Similar improvements have boosted results at S&W's much smaller plant in Houlton, Maine, which has the distinction of being America's leading producer of handcuffs.

Prepared for resistance to his plans, Golden found exactly the opposite. "It was an organization hungry for change," he told me. Employees, many of whom were also stockholders, had seen the stock price tank, and they knew the company was in trouble. Even when he hired new executives and imported all sorts of best practices from other industries, the employees seemed to understand and accept them. Part of the credit goes to Golden's insistence that his top people follow in his footsteps, literally, and take regular strolls through the factory to talk and listen attentively to his workers.

"I think we've succeeded in creating an environment where people know we will listen to them," he says. "I don't have all the answers, and I don't spend a lot of time in my office with the door shut because I get bored. I'm a walk-around kind of guy." On his walks, he carries a pad and a pen, and when someone has a problem or a suggestion, he writes it down and follows through.

For employees, S&W's impressive growth rate is a blessing on many levels, not least of which is job security. The increased productivity achieved through investment in up-to-date manufacturing techniques and equipment normally leads to shrinking payrolls, but Smith & Wesson has actually been adding jobs to meet growing demand for its products, new and old. It is, in Golden's words, "the perfect scenario."

I was curious about whether Wal-Mart was an S&W customer. As it happens, the giant retailer doesn't sell handguns, although it does sell Thompson/Center rifles. But the question led Golden to recall his own experience with Wal-Mart when he worked at Kohler. "What I learned was that there are ways to do business with big guys on your own terms when you have a brand," he told me. "The reality is that Home Depot needs Kohler's plumbing in their stores as much as Kohler needs Home Depot. At Smith & Wesson, we have the brand, too."

"WHAT I LEARNED WAS THAT THERE ARE WAYS TO DO BUSINESS WITH BIG GUYS ON YOUR OWN TERMS WHEN YOU HAVE A BRAND."

Golden is intent on making the most of S&W's powerful brand. "I think we would be cheating the shareholders and the employees if we didn't enhance the brand," he says. "But my number one responsibility is to protect it." So far, he's done amazingly well on both counts.

GET SMART

> ► *Hunt (the right) heads.* Big corporate change is top-down driven. When a company is in trouble, the change might need to begin at the top. But boards tread cautiously when deciding to replace a CEO. A wrong move could put the company at even further risk.
>
> Smith & Wesson's directors showed courage: first, in taking action; second, for recognizing Golden's qualities; and, third, for ignoring the reasons for which some might have considered him inappropriate. I normally advise a board to look for a CEO with deep expertise in the company's industry. Some boards naïvely believe that if an executive has done well in one business, he or she can do well in another. Some examples of cross-industry success exist, but they are few and far between. An executive's deep knowledge of an industry is important, especially if the recovery or reinvention of a business is required.

Golden, however, had the perfect set of experiences—in both manufacturing and turnarounds—to prepare for the challenges at Smith & Wesson. He also had the right management style for the job—an appetite for performance excellence and, at the same time, a respect for the people at S&W. This board saw Golden's qualities, did its job, and chose well.

▶ *Find what's truly valuable.* When you are making a big change in a company, it is critical to know what assets you can leverage and what assets you need to protect. Golden knew that Smith & Wesson was a much-respected name in the gun world. He could have left it there and focused solely on bringing the company's sales and production operations into the twenty-first century. Instead he insisted on extensive research to uncover what he perceived to be S&W's (and any company's) most valuable asset—its brand. What he found helped him to make a sharp turn in S&W's course, with most impressive results. If he hadn't asked, he might never have fully grasped just how potent the brand was and could be. Brand management was a skill he picked up at Kohler.

The other asset that Golden saw was the S&W people. Generations of families had worked at the Springfield plant. The people were skilled and loyal—and, most important, they would do whatever it took to bring the company back to life. He treated these people with great respect, and they returned the sentiment. It was palpable as I walked through the plant.

- *Squeeze nickels.* I'm a strong believer that a company must be a low-cost producer to compete. That's independent of its profits and the demand for its products. Being efficient today is table stakes. We are in a long-term cycle of dramatic productivity improvement across all industries, and if you don't keep up, you will soon be out of the game.

I'M A STRONG BELIEVER THAT A COMPANY MUST BE A LOW-COST PRODUCER TO COMPETE.

When Golden was at Stanley Works, he worked for John Trani, a member of Jack Welch's team at General Electric. Trani had absorbed Welch's penchant for holding down costs. Golden learned that lesson well and practiced it at S&W, introducing new manufacturing techniques to reduce expenses and raise productivity. But he combined his understanding of dollars and cents with a skill acquired at Black & Decker: demand creation. The combination produced simultaneous high productivity and job creation. For any company, cutting costs while raising demand creates the ideal conditions for success. It signals to employees that getting efficient and cutting costs doesn't necessarily mean that they will lose their jobs.

- *Walk and talk.* There's no magic formula for being a successful chief executive. Golden had the intelligence and business training to make a lot of the right moves in terms of reorganizing the sales force, hiring talented aides, and leveraging the brand. I suspect, though, that he and his company would not be where they are today had he not possessed something no corporate experience could give him: a dual personality. By that, I mean he was both a no-nonsense, results-oriented boss and an empathic, open-minded leader—a walk-around guy. In my experience, if you want to inspire people, there's nothing more effective than the presence of the chief in their midst, face to face, listening to what they say and being ready to act on it.

QUESTIONS TO ASK YOURSELF

▶ If you are trying to revive or redirect your company, do you have the right management team at the top?

▶ What skills and management style does your executive team require?

▶ If you have an active board of directors, does it understand your condition and opportunities?

▶ What are your company's principle assets—not just real estate and capital, but brand, intellectual property, and people?

▶ How can you leverage these assets to drive accelerated growth?

▶ If your business is not performing well, where are the breakdowns occurring and what management disciplines must you apply to fix your systemic problems?

▶ Are you a low-cost producer and, if not, how are you going to get there?

▶ Are you walking the "factory floor"?

JEFFREY HOUSENBOLD WAS
AN EBAY VICE PRESIDENT
WITH AN MBA FROM
HARVARD. HIS WIFE HAD
EARNED AN MBA, TOO—
FROM EQUALLY PRESTIGIOUS
WHARTON—AND SHE HAD
A HIGH-POWERED JOB TO
MATCH. THEY WERE ALSO
RAISING THREE SONS UNDER
THE AGE OF FIVE, A FULL-
TIME JOB ALL BY ITSELF.

CHAPTER 5

COMPETE BY CHANGING YOUR FRAME OF REFERENCE: HOW SHUTTERFLY SAW THE BIGGER PICTURE

Predictably, what the Housenbolds never had enough of was time—especially the time to share life's pleasures and to enjoy watching their kids grow. "Between her schedule and mine, I barely had time to talk to her, my kids, my mom, or anyone else outside business," Housenbold confesses. But Housenbold and his wife found a way to capture special moments and share them with friends and family through photography and a web site, Shutterfly.com, that makes it easy to spread the joy around. "We spent $1,900 on Shutterfly prints," Housenbold told me, "and that was the year before I even worked there!"

Housenbold became CEO of Shutterfly, based in Redwood City, California, in January 2005. At the time, the company, which Dan Baum and Eva Manolis had founded in December 1999, billed itself as just an online photo finisher. But within two years, Housenbold had turned Shutterfly into something much bigger and smarter—an Internet-based social-expression and personal-publishing service that helps consumers "share life's joys, stay connected, and preserve memories." Shutterfly still prints customers' photographs from old-style 35mm cameras as well as digital equipment, but now the site also offers a range of personalized products and services that fit its new strategic vision. Customers can get personalized greeting cards, scrapbooks, collage posters, photo books, calendars, personalized stationary, and much more, plus a range of services that make it easy to upload, edit, enhance, touch up, share, and store their digital photos.

Housenbold had found one of the prime secrets of business growth: changing his business's frame of reference to expand its identity and compete on a new and much larger field.

By transcending the product boundaries of an online photo finisher, he could not only survive trends in the photo industry that were decimating some of his competitors, but he also could turn those changes into his own advantage. And he could use his new status to exploit larger trends that touched only incidentally on photography. It's a neat and impressive trick, as if a gazelle being chased by cheetahs were to suddenly morph into a lion.

HOUSENBOLD HAD FOUND ONE OF THE PRIME SECRETS OF BUSINESS GROWTH: CHANGING HIS BUSINESS'S FRAME OF REFERENCE TO EXPAND ITS IDENTITY AND COMPETE ON A NEW AND MUCH LARGER FIELD.

Talking with Housenbold reminded me of a well-known company that hired me early in my consulting career. Hallmark, the first name in greeting cards, was one of my early process-reengineering clients. When I arrived at its headquarters in Kansas City, Missouri, the company's executives told me that Hallmark was *not* a greeting-card company, but a social-expressions company. Changing the frame of reference had enabled Hallmark to expand the range of products with which its customers could convey their messages. Hallmark wasn't just about cards anymore; now it offered stuffed animals, porcelain figurines, books, pens—any product that could convey feelings between people. Housenbold used the same phrase, "social expressions," but he expanded it brilliantly: Shutterfly's new frame of reference stretched beyond consumer goods to include the concept of an online community.

Housenbold's insight called for a complete makeover of
Shutterfly, which led to a sales explosion. In fiscal year 2007
alone, revenues are projected to increase 45 to 50 percent, to
more than $138 million. The company was on track to reach 7
million orders in calendar year 2007, a 37 percent jump from
5.1 million in 2006 and nearly double the 3.6 million orders
received in 2005.

When Housenbold arrived at Shutterfly, he brought with him
a proven record for integrating the interests of commerce
and community. At the Raging Bull financial web site, where
Housenbold worked as chief operating officer, he had been
determined to level the playing field for the individual investor.
As general manager of the AltaVista search engine, Housenbold
worked to make knowledge available to everyone. And at eBay,
he focused on helping "the little guys" compete effectively with
global corporations.

Housenbold discovered the makings of a solid community at
Shutterfly. Its clients are amazingly loyal—77 percent of the
company's revenue came from active customers, who currently
number more than two million. Clearly, these folks care deeply
about preserving and sharing their photographic memories.
With that information in hand, Housenbold reimagined
the company's frame of reference, expanding it from photo
finishing to a full range of products and services to facilitate
taking photos, editing and packaging them, posting them for
friends to enjoy and critique, and exchanging tools and tips
with other Shutterfly members. This metamorphosis greatly
enhanced the customers' enjoyment and sharply differentiated
the company from its competitors. Housenbold saw Shutterfly

ρ Digital camera
Digital cameras were
supposed to put an end to
the printed picture. The
opposite occurred.

ρ 35mm film
Housenbold saw how digital
media could be transformed
into multiple forms of social
expression, connecting
communities large and small.

through a wider lens that took in new trends
in the photo industry and society at large.

When I asked Housenbold to explain
Shutterfly's extraordinary growth rate, he
began modestly by crediting a rising tide
that is lifting all boats. Photo finishing, he
noted, was an $11 billion market in the
United States in 2005, and it is expected to
nearly triple to $31 billion in 2009. That is
a sensational rise all by itself, but it's even
more sensational in light of contradictory
predictions made by supposedly
knowledgeable experts not so long ago.

I'm always amused when economic seers hail
some future phenomenon that never comes
to pass. Remember how the computer was
going to create a paperless society? Instead,
paper consumption soared. Similarly, the
prophets predicted that the arrival of the
digital camera would decimate the demand
for prints. Again, just the opposite happened.
In the past, amateur photographers would
print a whole roll of 24 or 36 exposures

taken at a family party, on a vacation, or at some other event. We shutterbugs didn't have much choice because most of us had no way of knowing what was worth printing on a roll until the whole thing was processed. Who hasn't thrown away dozens, if not hundreds, of pictures that were blurry, badly framed (someone's head got cut off), or just plain unflattering and not worth saving? But because of the cost of developing photos, we rationed the number of times we clicked the shutter. Today, with digital cameras and the ability to preview pictures, amateur photographers might take hundreds of shots and choose 50 to print. That's twice as many as a roll of film in the old days.

But the unexpected boom in photo printing doesn't fully explain Shutterfly's rapid growth. These days, photo printing isn't even the company's main revenue source. No, the real bonanza came from Housenbold's reimagined vision for the organization. He recognized a major consumer trend and adapted his company's strategy and business model to exploit it.

Americans have never been hungrier for individual expression, new ways of saying, "Here I am." In 2006, we spent an estimated $6 billion just to equip our cell phones with special ring tones. People are blogging, podcasting, YouTubing, and MySpacing by the tens of millions. Neilsen/Net Ratings reported a 47 percent year-over-year increase, to 68.8 million users, at the top 10 social-networking sites in April 2006. People are also flocking to sites where they can list items they own and products they wish they owned.

Housenbold understood what was going on, and he had the foresight to see how people's need to connect with others in personalized settings could reinvigorate the photo business. Accordingly, he introduced dozens of ways in which Shutterfly customers could turn their photos into personalized objects of expression. His customers can now put their images on greeting cards and calendars, coffee mugs and T-shirts, magnets and jewelry. They can publish their own bound books with personalized text and photographs, or weave favorite photos of their child into a 40-page copy of *My Adventure on Sesame Street.* With the site's photo-editing tools, they can remove people from a photo and whiten the teeth of everyone remaining.

Housenbold envisioned Shutterfly as the premium lifestyle brand in the online photo-finishing business. His goal was to make it the easiest-to-use site with the most design choices and an unbending dedication to customer service. Unlike some of its competitors, Shutterfly bans high-pressure sales tactics, doesn't delete stored photos if a customer disappears for a while, and doesn't compress images, reducing resolution to save money. Shutterfly's prices are not the lowest, although they are competitive. Its customer service, however, ranks as the industry's best, and its clients are more than willing to pay for it.

But even as he widened his lens, Housenbold stayed focused on his primary business. By resisting the temptation to branch out from its photographic base, Shutterfly has succeeded in building a premium brand and maintaining and expanding a trusting customer base. And the loyalty it enjoys has facilitated its lateral move into the scrapbook, greeting-card, and photo-publishing fields.

Many of the company's innovations have sprung directly from Housenbold's finely tuned sense of community. Customers can create two personal web pages, for example, each with an address they choose, where friends and relatives can view and upload photos for everyone to enjoy and even make comments about them. To build community, Housenbold has introduced numerous photo contests involving pets, family reunions, hometowns, and school spirit, with Shutterfly products as prizes. But instead of offering big money and risk commercializing the experience, he shrewdly decided to keep the prizes familial and modest.

Housenbold's sense of community extends to his employees, whom he views as fellow innovators, not just nine-to-fivers. Anyone with an idea is encouraged to submit a simple business-case presentation, and people from all over the organization share their brainstorms. Each idea is judged in terms of potential economic return and resource requirements. High-level screeners meet regularly to choose the winners.

When I spoke with Housenbold, he was about to join one such meeting to consider 13 ideas that had been winnowed from 85. He explained the workings of the process this way: "Let's pretend someone proposes to roll out a new photo product, a picture on a tie for Father's Day. We'll ask, 'Would it help us differentiate? Is it on brand? Will it be in tune with our quality? What kind of investment would be required? Would it help smooth out our seasonality? How much demand would there be? How much would it cannibalize our other products?'"

Having this process in place has enabled the company to tap the fresh ideas brought by new people hired during the expansion of the last two years. Furthermore, the widespread organizational input has clarified workforce thinking, Housenbold told me. "There's a shared belief that focusing on three to five ideas which will allow us to truly differentiate is the right approach to winning in the marketplace."

Housenbold acknowledges that his leadership style requires a greater investment of up-front time and energy than a less formal approach would demand. "But I think it makes for better decisions," he says, "and it allows decisions to be communicated and buy-in to happen in a much deeper way throughout the organization." It also means that Housenbold has to build flexibility into his budget, allocating 10 to 15 percent for "trying things" such as a new go-to-market strategy or a new partnership. A certain number of failures are to be expected, he says, but "it's the portfolio of those experiences that hopefully will lead us to learn and grow."

Partnerships and affiliations play a major part in Shutterfly's growth strategy. In the first half of 2007, the company forged agreements with Yahoo!, Sony, Delta Airlines, Target, and David's Bridal stores that include mutual promotional efforts and special customer offers. Target, for instance, will display Shutterfly photo books and greeting cards, and customers will be able to order prints online and pick them up at the stores an hour later.

When Dan Baum and Eva Manolis started Shutterfly, most of their start-up money came from Jim Clark, who had presided at the creation of Netscape, Healtheon, and Silicon Graphics, where Baum and Manolis had worked. But the new venture struggled for years, weighed down by a sour economy, the high-tech bust, and the inroads made by competitors such as Snapfish and Ofoto. When asked what kept Shutterfly going, Clark replied, "I did. It was a matter of money. I kept reinvesting. I don't like to give up." He served as board chairman until January 2007.

Shutterfly began turning a profit in 2003, but by then the digital photo-printing market was splintering. Offline retailers such as Wal-Mart and Walgreens had jumped into the act, along with online giants AOL and Google.

ρ **Target**
Even Internet-based businesses use multiple bricks-and-mortar channels to reach as many customers as possible.

Meanwhile, older rivals Snapfish and Ofoto were acquired by two deep-pocketed expansionists, Hewlett-Packard and Kodak. The future looked pretty bleak when Housenbold arrived with his wide-lens vision that would shift the frame of reference from photo finishing to social expression and community.

Housenbold's performance was not a one-man show, of course. Others contributed their ideas. But it was Housenbold's ability to view the company in a broader context that encompassed societal trends and provided the springboard for Shutterfly's hugely successful reincarnation.

GET SMART

▶ *Look at the bigger picture.* How is your business defined, and how do its parameters fit into your industry? How is the industry changing, and how can you change your frame of reference to compete on a wider field where you could develop an edge?

In some industries (airlines and automakers come to mind), business leaders, perhaps distracted by brand fame and a false sense of ownership, have lost touch with their customers' needs. A determined person can seize such an opportunity by asking, what is this industry about? What do people want from their cars or their airline flights, how is that changing, and what special capabilities does the company have to give them what they want? An expanded frame of reference might suggest a new service, such as to provide in-flight travel updates or car rentals by the hour to city dwellers (sorry, Zipcar got there first).

The magnitude of the opportunity in the auto industry was brought home to me recently when a group of Japanese auto executives discussed their corporate strategy. Their design, manufacturing, marketing, and business processes are all driven by one simple idea— building cars that consumers will love. That is hardly a novel idea. But the U.S. auto industry seems to have lost sight of that goal. A world of growth is open to the company that figures out what makes a car lovable today.

▶ *Build a community, but tend to business.* The Internet is awash in businesses that built communities to feed the emotional or practical needs of their members. Doing good for people is eminently desirable, and there's nothing more exciting than standing at the intersection of community and commerce. Too often, though, these businesses fail to follow through on the second half of the equation.

Commerce is about making money. An emotional appeal is powerful and communities can create meaningful connections, but you can't earn a profit unless you have a differentiating strategy and an efficient business model. Shutterfly has both, which is why it is among the few online communities that earn their keep by selling real products and services.

Call me old-fashioned, but I am a fan of Internet-based businesses that deliver products and services to paying customers. How else can most companies expect to build sustainable businesses? A lot of supposedly smart venture money is flowing into community-based Internet businesses such as YouTube and Facebook, which derive their profits solely from advertising. Making money in this way might be a viable business model, but, in my opinion, few of these businesses will survive as profit-making ventures. A less risky business model includes marketing some of the thousands of products and services that can be sold to Internet communities. The ultimate proof of the value of a product or service is that someone is willing to pay for it. But you will need a laserlike focus and a good operating model to succeed in delivering products sold online. Shutterfly has achieved success through a fully integrated vertical operation.

THE ULTIMATE PROOF OF THE VALUE OF A PRODUCT OR SERVICE IS THAT SOMEONE IS WILLING TO PAY FOR IT.

▶ *Widen your lens, but narrow your focus.* Housenbold and I agree that the Internet favors a pure play, a company devoted to only one line of business. The sites that focus on a single market do better than those that spread themselves around, no matter how big they are. Compare Monster.com's recruiting success to that of your local newspaper, where job openings are advertised along with dozens of other services. Or how about eBay's online auctions versus Yahoo!'s? A narrowly focused organization can channel its resources and energies more efficiently. That helps explain Shutterfly's success. Financial markets also favor pure-play businesses; they perform better in the long run.

A NARROWLY FOCUSED ORGANIZATION CAN
CHANNEL ITS RESOURCES AND ENERGIES MORE
EFFICIENTLY.

▶ *Organize for ideas.* Just because ideas are ephemeral
doesn't mean you can't apply the same kind of rigorous
management attention to idea generation that you apply
to product packaging. The ability to view your company
in a new frame of reference is not limited to the executive
ranks. Shutterfly has created a culture that puts a high
value on employee suggestions. Employees know that
their ideas can improve the company's bottom line, which
benefits all players. They also realize that their ideas will
be taken seriously, studied, and measured against known
standards—and if an idea works, they will be rewarded. Of
course, every employee hopes his or her suggestion will be
adopted, but, as Housenbold explains, a negative decision
doesn't frustrate people as much as failing to understand
how decisions get made. The obvious solution is to make
sure the process is transparent to everyone.

In working on this book, I found that most high-growth
companies have adopted some form of process to capture
ideas from the front lines. Some of these processes are
formal, employing the techniques set forth in the Kaizen
and quality movements. Others are less formal, with ideas
bubbling up from below. Generally, all ideas are quickly
tested. The good ones survive; the bad ones are put to rest,
but with respect.

▶ *Persist in your quest.* It takes courage to move out of your familiar boundaries and play a bigger game on a new field. If your company has been around for a while, your audacious behavior might feel very risky. But success belongs only to those with the courage to stand by their convictions and risk failure all the way. Even in an imperfect world, the good guys do win. So keep your faith as well as your head. Surely there were doubters who snickered when Housenbold proposed recasting Shutterfly around the concept of community.

AFTER YOU'VE THOUGHT DEEPLY ABOUT A BIG IDEA YOUR COMPANY CAN EXECUTE, AND AFTER YOU'VE VERIFIED JUST HOW SLEEPY YOUR COMPETITION IS, DON'T LET ANYONE TALK YOU OUT OF CHARGING AHEAD. PURSUING BIG IDEAS REQUIRES PERSISTENCE.

After you've thought deeply about a big idea your company can execute, and after you've verified just how sleepy your competition is, don't let anyone talk you out of charging ahead. Pursuing big ideas requires persistence.

QUESTIONS TO ASK YOURSELF

▶ Can you see an opportunity to meet a neglected need by widening your company's frame of reference? What will give you an edge in this expanded playing field?

- ▶ How does your idea fit your capabilities? How does it relate to the trends in your industry and in the broader society?

- ▶ Do you believe strongly enough in your idea to risk failure?

- ▶ Is your idea compelling enough to entice others in your company to join you?

- ▶ Do you have a sound and workable plan for generating profits in the near term?

- ▶ Is the focus of your business narrow enough to enable you to target markets and build the capabilities needed to serve those markets?

- ▶ Do you have processes in place to harvest ideas from your people and integrate them into your business model?

DAN JOHNSON AND MIKE CAPPELLO ARE ENGINEERS. THEY MET BACK IN THE EARLY 1980S, WHEN THEY BOTH WORKED IN NUCLEAR ENERGY FOR THE PUBLIC SERVICE COMPANY OF COLORADO AT THE FORT ST. VRAIN NUCLEAR POWER PLANT. THEY ARE ALSO FRIENDS, THE KIND WHO NEVER LOSE TOUCH. SO WHEN THEY SET OFF IN DIFFERENT DIRECTIONS IN THE EARLY 1990S, IT WAS ALMOST INEVITABLE THAT THEIR PATHS WOULD CONVERGE AGAIN.

CHAPTER 6

Compete by Doing Everything Yourself: S.A. Robotics— Reaching Into Every Detail

And they did—in an enterprise perched at the crucial nexus of science and ecology, but with a decidedly twenty-first-century twist on an old-fashioned business model: Their company does everything for itself.

After Public Service Company of Colorado, Cappello took on assorted project management assignments in a variety of industries, including nuclear energy. Some involved cleaning up Cold War era nuclear waste. Johnson stayed in Loveland, Colorado, and started a company in 1992 called Special Application Robotics, which made tools that could substitute for humans in the dismantling of nuclear reactors. His first project as a Westinghouse subcontractor was to chop up the reactor at the Fort St. Vrain power plant in the shadow of the Colorado Rockies, a plant where he had once worked as superintendent. Fort St. Vrain was the first

ρ **Nuclear plant**
Some markets that appear challenging can provide extraordinary opportunity for people with both the appetite and the necessary skills.

commercial nuclear-generating plant in the United States to be decommissioned, and Johnson was sure it wouldn't be the last.

By spring 2003, Cappello was looking for a new passion. Meanwhile, Johnson's company, originally staffed by him and his wife, had outgrown his Loveland garage and was now a 12-person operation designing and creating impressive new technology in a variety of areas. But with revenues having topped out at $1.2 million in 2001, S.A. Robotics was deeply in debt and Johnson's bankers were growing impatient. Forced to seek help, Johnson found it in his old friend Cappello.

Friendship aside, Cappello saw enormous potential in the work Johnson's company was doing. But he also saw the need for a drastic transformation in the way the company was organized and operated. Determined to help, Cappello literally bet the ranch—his family's 960-acre Colorado ranch served as primary collateral—to become co-owner and chief executive of S.A. Robotics. Within four years, revenues had skyrocketed 2000 percent to greater than $17 million a year, the workforce had expanded to 140, and the company was fighting off venture capital investors.

Though Cappello is now in charge, the company's success has been a joint effort. It was Johnson who had the initial vision and Cappelo who had the new vision. Together they saw the opportunity others overlooked in the design and manufacture of customized robots for the decommissioning of nuclear plants and for similarly dangerous work in other settings. And it was Cappello whose drive and organizational skills led the company to reshape the way it performs its tasks. Virtually from the moment he arrived, Cappello told me, he insisted on bringing every aspect of the operation back into the company.

This chapter celebrates the rare and stubborn breed of leaders such as Cappello who have bucked the outsourcing wave of the past two decades and outsmarted their rivals by doing everything themselves. Although some manufacturing companies joined the stampede to outsourcing because they lacked the equipment or know-how to handle a particular task on their own, the typical impetus for farming out work was simply basic cost cutting. In theory, outsourcing is a positive—a company can reduce expenses while maintaining long-distance control and, in some cases, benefit from the expertise of its partners. But when a company's product must be tailor-made

ρ **Robot**
Machines will never replace people, but some actually do a better job than we humans—and keep us safe from harm.

© S.A. Robotics. Reprinted with permission.

for each customer, or when it must meet exacting standards, outsourcing might be the wrong way to go.

S.A. Robotics falls into both categories. Its custom remote-control robots are designed to exacting standards that keep people safe as they perform the deadly work of deactivating, decontaminating, and dismantling nuclear and other hazardous-waste facilities. The robots, some of which are 100 feet long and cost as much as $2 million, are tailor-made to operate perfectly in a variety of hellish conditions pertinent to each type of job. If they break down, no one can go in to get them and take them out to be repaired. In other words, there is no room for error. "We are the Orange County Choppers shop of the industry," says Harley-Davidson fan Cappello of his business model.

The company also builds systems to contain and otherwise handle dangerous waste materials, including petrochemicals, and it designs and manufactures process equipment such as gloveboxes for industrial and nuclear applications. (For the uninitiated, gloveboxes are sealed containers that enable a person to manipulate objects in a different atmosphere by inserting his or her hands into gloves incorporated into the unit.) One of the company's more unique products is a robotic arm that will remotely clean up the third worst nuclear accident in the world at the Pile 1 reactor at windscale in the United Kingdom.

Admittedly, in this era of outsourcing, the one-stop-shop business model seems old-fashioned, a throwback to the days when vertical integration was all the rage. Standard Oil Company controlled every drop of fuel from the wellhead to the gas pump, and Ford Motor previously owned all its processes from the steel mill to the car lot. But in recent years, under pressure from Wall Street to churn out ever greater productivity and double-digit growth, the corporate world has reversed course, rushing to farm out all but the most essential tasks to outside specialists. Indeed, outsourcing has become so ubiquitous that some of the most storied national brands now decorate goods produced anywhere but in their home countries. The extent of outsourcing became both obvious and embarrassing during the 2007 uproar over dangerous toys and food from China.

For a company to do it all, however, a great deal of internal discipline and substantial capital investment in labor-saving machinery and software is needed. This also requires a full measure of ingenuity and courage.

When I asked Cappello why he was so determined to make S.A. Robotics independent of outside suppliers, he replied, "I guess I'm a contrarian, always riding against what the rest of the world is doing. And I'm old school—I want to control everything." All the jobs that were subcontracted out when he joined the company—for example, software code writing and the supply of high-tech raw materials such as carbon fiber—are now in-house capabilities. And at a time when many major corporations are busily shedding their in-house R&D capabilities, S.A. Robotics is designing and manufacturing its own technology. That way, the company can be sure that everything that goes into its products is up to the stringent demands of the hard and perilous work they are made to do.

Cappello also likes knowing that his personal success or failure, as well as that of the company, is not in the hands of outsiders. "I can't subject myself to being a victim," he told me. "If I promise a customer a delivery, I don't want it to depend on some subcontractor coming through with his piece of it. It goes against every bone in my body." His take-control instinct has been bolstered by financial concerns. Many of the company's projects are performed on a hard-money, fixed-price basis delivered on accelerated schedules. An unexpected cost increase or a failure to deliver what was promised in a timely manner could turn profits into losses.

About half of S.A. Robotics's revenue comes from its nuclear work. One such project, at the Rancho Seco nuclear power plant in Clay Station, California, required the company to build a remote water-jet cutting system that would take apart a "hot" reactor with 17-inch-thick carbon steel walls. The company

also designed and built a remote-controlled system to retrieve the water and debris produced in the cutting process. Elsewhere, at the Hanford Tank Farms in the state of Washington, the site of 177 underground storage tanks filled with radioactive and chemical waste, S.A. Robotics created a remote-controlled surveillance system consisting of a camera assembly with a self-cleaning lens and a sealed camera arm that retracts into a housing for maintenance purposes. The complexity and scope of the company's projects make it easy to understand why Cappello insists on maintaining control of all the pieces.

Part of the company's meteoric growth, as Cappello readily acknowledges, can be attributed to the public's post-9/11 concern about the use—or, rather, misuse—of radioactive materials by terrorists, and the massive, government-funded cleanup of Cold War–era nuclear waste sites. At the same time, the insurance industry, battered by rising workers' compensation costs, has been campaigning against allowing employees to work in dangerous environments, sending one customer after another into the arms of S.A. Robotics.

Johnson and Cappello have welcomed them with products that meet the daunting challenge of operating untended for as long as the job requires. S.A. Robotics is certified by the International Organization for Standardization (ISO), Cappello says, "but our systems have to live up to a higher-than-ISO standard. We analyze materials down to the molecular level. We have taken commercially sold electric motors and rewired them so they can withstand the high radiation environments."

With every conceivable operation required to turn out the robots contained within the plant walls, a visitor to S.A.

Colorado State University

There's nothing like having a special relationship with a university to better enable you to find bright young minds.

𝒫 colorado state university

Robotics can experience the whole process, from design to the shop floor, to the product test facility, to the shipping department. "Our customers love it," Cappello told me. "Most of them are middle-level technical managers. Just about every other engineering firm has spun off any fabrication capability, so when these guys come here, they're blown away."

The company's success would have been impossible if it hadn't been able to hire and retain talented, highly motivated employees. Location helps: The headquarters stands between Colorado State University in Fort Collins and the University of Colorado in Boulder. To prime the pump, the company established an internship program with Colorado State. "We've had engineers who interned with us for four years of college," he says, "and when they graduated, they rolled right in and hit the ground running." They stick around, too—Cappello boasts that the company has a near zero attrition rate.

That doesn't happen because of the pay level, which he describes as "middle road." He keeps his people happy by encouraging them to speak their mind, giving them a chance to work on challenging projects from start to finish, and making them feel like important parts of a proud, can-do culture. "Around here, nobody is bored and hanging around the water cooler," he says. Having all that extraordinary talent under one roof gives the company another edge in doing everything for itself. "When it's time to deliver a project, everybody's running around with their hair on fire and everybody's involved," Cappello says. "The engineers are in the shop helping the fab guys build the stuff— whatever has to be done is done." The company has about five or six projects going at any given time.

The company provides some perks, of course. Unlike many companies these days, S.A. Robotics pays for employees' health insurance, and it has also set up a 401(k) program. Indicative perhaps of its close-knit workforce and in line with its old-fashioned business model, the company follows some simple but unusual practices, such as giving each employee a birthday card and a gift certificate for a local restaurant. But Capello's people don't stay for perks. They stay because they are embarking on an important, worthwhile mission, cleaning up some of the world's worst environmental messess and making work safer for nuclear employees.

Cappello is no softy, though. After he took over as CEO, the company went through a winnowing process. "We had a lot of communication issues," he says, "and personal agendas got in the way of what was right for the company. We lost some jobs. I made some key personnel changes—I had the wrong people in the wrong seats—and we flattened out."

Extra discipline is required when a company operates with
fixed-price deals; the staff has to understand a customer's
needs and simply must stay on schedule and on price. That can
sometimes be a challenge with engineers. "They get to talking
with one of the customer's engineers, and the next thing you
know, they've decided to add a little feature," Cappello says.
"But then they forget to go back to the shop and make sure the
cost of the little feature gets covered."

Alluding to the fact that S.A. Robotics has just two shareholders
(Johnson and Cappello), Cappello is proud to note, "What we
have here is a very capital-intensive business going through an
exponential growth with absolutely no injection capital. All the
growth was funded out of operating revenues." When I asked if
he had ever been approached by venture capitalists, Cappello
said that after the company began receiving awards and honors
(the *Inc.* 500)—Cappello was a finalist for the Ernst & Young
Entrepreneur of the Year award, among other things—his phone
never stopped ringing with offers of cash and buyouts. "We're a
perfect candidate," he points out. "We have a great technology
and growing IT portfolio. We do all our own patent prep work.
We have good, clean, well-diversified end products."

Would he and Johnson sell a minority stake, or even the whole
company? Yes, Cappello replied, but only to the right partner.
"I would want them to look at S.A. Robotics as a value added to
something they already have in the marketplace," he explains,
not someone coming in to spin off pieces of the company
and dismantle the one-stop shop. "My number one focus is to
build a sustainable company that every one of my youngest
employees can retire from."

"MY NUMBER ONE FOCUS IS TO BUILD A
SUSTAINABLE COMPANY THAT EVERY ONE OF MY
YOUNGEST EMPLOYEES CAN RETIRE FROM."

The company's future looks especially promising in Europe,
where its British projects already account for half its revenue.
"They have much tighter restrictions over there on worker safety
than we do, so they have just latched on to us with sole-source
contract after sole-source contract," Cappello says. Better
yet, some of the deals are structured as time-and-material
agreements, providing a steady stream of cash flow that the
company's usual fixed-price contracts don't provide. Cappello
also hopes to play a role in deactivating nuclear sites in the
former Eastern Block countries and also in Germany, which has
recently voted to shut down all its nuclear power plants.

GET SMART

- ► *Control what matters.* Doing everything yourself speaks
  to a very human impulse. When Cappello talked to me
  about his need to control his company's processes, I
  immediately understood that he was really talking about
  his distaste for losing control, especially for the kind of
  product he makes.

  If you manufacture a complex, customized product,
  the need for control is clear. If you are providing a more
  commoditized product or service, however, outsourcing
  part of your work might be a legitimate option or, in some
  cases, a competitive necessity. An outsourcing partner

⌒ S.A. Robotics factory

S.A. Robotics is highly
integrated. Its people have
the satisfaction of building
the product from beginning
to end. It is also the only
business I know of that can
boast near zero attrition.

might be able to do some of your work better, faster, and cheaper—and might also bring industry know-how and capabilities that will improve your product or service.

The key is to know what you are really good at, what makes you distinctive, and therefore, what you need to keep in-house. S.A. Robotics's distinctiveness hinges on its ability to produce highly complex and highly dependable pieces of robotic equipment. Thus, the company must oversee every detail of its manufacturing processes and maintain as much control over the design and fabrication as possible. Such a strategy typically comes at a high cost, but in the nuclear and petroleum industries, the cost of failure can be even higher.

THE KEY IS TO KNOW WHAT YOU ARE REALLY GOOD AT, WHAT MAKES YOU DISTINCTIVE, AND THEREFORE, WHAT YOU NEED TO KEEP IN-HOUSE.

© S.A. Robotics. Reprinted with permission.

I could write another book on what to do if you decide that
outsourcing is a viable or required part of your strategy.
Many books already have been written on the subject.
But here is one important piece of advice: If you decide to
outsource the manufacturing of a particular component
or an entire process, don't pick your outsourcing partner
on the basis of price alone. Make sure that your partner
shares your business values and priorities. With this
shared perspective, you're far less likely to have problems
with quality, scheduling, or communication.

MAKE SURE THAT YOUR PARTNER SHARES YOUR BUSINESS VALUES AND PRIORITIES.

▶ *Hire the best and keep them.* Turnover is the bane of
every company's existence. A company might spend
huge amounts of time, energy, and cash on developing
an employee and patiently putting up with the
inevitable tensions, only to have that employee suddenly
disappear—and end up working for a competitor. These
days, with technical people in high demand all around
the globe, they have their pick of jobs and can flit with
abandon from one to another. That S.A. Robotics has
managed to achieve near zero attrition is a tribute to the
culture Cappello and Johnson have put in place and to
the high-quality work he provides his people. He doesn't
pay his engineers extraordinary sums, and the perks
provided are not particularly special. What keeps people
on the job is the chance to do interesting, challenging

work; to see it through to conclusion; and to be recognized as contributing members of a community of dedicated, results-oriented people.

I sit on the compensation committee of two enterprises—one is a public company, the other a university. Both are deeply involved in technology. Because these organizations attract and develop extraordinary people, they are targeted by competitors as a source of talent. I learned a long time ago that a competitor is always willing to pay more for the best people. But what makes great people stay put is not their compensation, but a love of their work and the values that they share with their colleagues. A few individuals will sell themselves for higher pay—and a company or university must have competitive compensation—but the best people remain committed to an enterprise that has both a high sense of purpose and meaningful work to be performed.

I LEARNED A LONG TIME AGO THAT A COMPETITOR IS ALWAYS WILLING TO PAY MORE FOR THE BEST PEOPLE. BUT WHAT MAKES GREAT PEOPLE STAY PUT IS NOT THEIR COMPENSATION, BUT A LOVE OF THEIR WORK AND THE VALUES THAT THEY SHARE WITH THEIR COLLEAGUES.

▶ *Don't build to sell.* The venture world is filled with people who talk about how to "monetize" what they are building. That's the jargon used to describe how they will cash out of the business. Often the founder of a company and its investors will make an early decision on its eventual disposition: Will it become a public company with the currency of liquid stock? Will it be merged with another company? Or might it just be sold for cash? It's a legitimate discussion for investors, but I prefer a business with a life and purpose of its own. Chances are, it will have a better shot at success over the long term. Speaking as an investor, I would never buy a company that was built just to be sold.

SPEAKING AS AN INVESTOR, I WOULD NEVER BUY A COMPANY THAT WAS BUILT JUST TO BE SOLD.

Although I talked with Cappello about S.A. Robotics' interest in a "strategic" investor, it is clear that Cappello and Johnson built their company to solve tough environmental problems. It was not built just to attract a buyer. I'm not saying that a buyer who is a good fit might not come along, but the acquisition and merger of small- or medium-sized companies is a risky game—for both the acquired and the acquirer. The acquirer needs to understand what it's buying, both how the company really operates and its culture. The acquired needs to understand that, no matter what's represented at the time of a sale, it is giving up control of the enterprise.

I learned this in a positive way when CSC acquired my own consulting firm. I described the sequence of those events in the introduction to this book. My tenure at CSC was fulfilling, and my company flourished within CSC for many years. That's because CSC's chairman and CEO understood the unique asset he had purchased and let me continue to run the company as it had been run.

The chairman and I had debates from time to time about certain issues—did I have to pay our senior consultants so much?—but, in the end, he left the important decisions to me. My company was never built to be sold, and that made it an even better asset for CSC.

QUESTIONS TO ASK YOURSELF

▶ Do you know the source of your distinctiveness? What do you do really well? What business processes must you continue to directly control?

▶ If you choose to outsource any part of your work, do you know who will do that work and the business values by which they operate?

▶ Is the work of your company designed to engage both the hearts and minds of your people? Are there ways to get more meaning back into the work of your company—to make that work more than a job?

▶ Do your people ever get to see the end result of what they produce, or meet the customer or end user?

▶ Are you building a company to keep? How are you ensuring its sustainability?

► If you believe that your business can prosper from having a strategic partner, do you really know that partner, and does that partner really know your company? Do you understand what each of you can bring to the table and how you will operate going forward?

► If finding a strategic partner is just the start of a process to sell out, you might be better off selling your business right now.

AT 32, JEFF GRADY WAS WASHED UP—A JOBLESS, ALMOST PENNILESS CASUALTY OF THE 2000 DOT-COM BUST, GOING NOWHERE IN DURHAM, NORTH CAROLINA. BETWEEN FRUITLESS JOB SEARCHES, HE SPENT HOURS AT THE GYM, SWEATING OUT HIS ANXIETIES. THEN HE DISCOVERED AN IRRESISTIBLE TOY, THE NEWLY INVENTED IPOD. HE HAD TO HAVE ONE.

CHAPTER 7

COMPETE BY TAPPING THE SUCCESS OF OTHERS: JIBBITZ WINS BY RIDING A CROC

In a burst of bravado and borrowing, he scrounged $399 and danced home with his treasure.

Eager to protect its shiny white surface and scratchable screen, he tried to buy a carrying case, but no such item existed. So Jeff made his own case out of plastic, using skills he had developed earlier as a sportswear designer. Eureka! His life changed. Other iPod owners admired his case and wanted their own.

Grady obliged: He refined the design of his case, found a manufacturer, started the company Digital Lifestyle Outfitters (DLI), launched a web site, and, within weeks, mastered a new specialty—supplying iPod owners with accessories that Apple itself had either overlooked or dismissed as unworthy of its techie brains. In 2006, selling 100 ancillary products—cases, remote controls,

ρ **Creating the need**
Revolutionary new products can create new consumer needs and wants. Sometimes, an enterprising consumer can turn those into a business.

boom boxes, and related gear—DLI grossed $84 million and moved to cheerful new quarters in laid-back Charleston, South Carolina. In three years, Jeff's company has grown by an astonishing 4,385 percent. That growth attracted the attention of Philips Electronics, which acquired DLI in 2007.

Every so often, a new product or old brand is so novel or exciting that it creates a groundswell, a mystique, a whole subcult of loyal customers avid to buy anything related to the sacred brand. At the luxury level, think Porsche, Rolex, Tiffany, Wedgewood, and Purdy shotguns. At another level, think Harley-Davidson, NASCAR, Budweiser, Silverado, the New England Patriots, and the U.S. Marine Corps. Such names become symbols, freighted with power and meaning for true believers. Some of their fans would happily wear the logos printed on their clothes, from caps to boxer shorts to sneakers. Some would—and many do—tattoo them right onto their skin.

One man's (or woman's) obsession is another's chance to outsmart the competition. People who identify with hot brands create secondary markets for businesspeople agile enough to piggyback on the original company's success. The payoff is growing; Grady is only one of the iPod accessory makers who are pulling in an estimated $1 billion in sales per year among them, and they are swooping down on new iPhone buyers to offer Apple-ripe gadgets, ranging from cases to docking stations. It's no game for the slow-footed. "Speed is extremely important," Grady emphasizes. "There's a big difference between being a leader and being a copycat. Being the first to market gives us the chance to test our product and see what works and what needs tweaking. Sometimes we have up to a year before the competition puts out a similar item, which means we have already moved on to a more sophisticated offering. We want to be constantly killing off our products."

"SPEED IS EXTREMELY IMPORTANT," GRADY EMPHASIZES. "THERE'S A BIG DIFFERENCE BETWEEN BEING A LEADER AND BEING A COPYCAT."

Piggybacking is not entirely free of risks, such as being squashed or stiffed by a big company whose success you're trying to complement with an ancillary product or service. After all, a shark doesn't necessarily welcome the pilot fish crowding its space. In the mid-1960s, for example, the inventor Robert Kearns came up with the intermittent windshield wiper, a mini-breakthrough in automotive history. Kearns patented the device and offered it to Detroit's Big Three automakers. They downplayed his idea and scoffed him out of town—then installed new intermittent wipers on all cars and trucks from then on. Kearns spent years and many thousands of dollars suing the automakers for patent infringement. When he finally won in the U.S. Supreme Court, the defendants were forced to pay him $30 million, a vindication soured by the near-certainty that he would have earned many times that amount in royalties had the automakers played straight with him.

However, piggybackers almost certainly benefit their target companies (and themselves) far more often than not. When a hot new product attracts a swarm of beneficial add-ons (accessories, decorations, extensions, enhancements, etc.), the resulting buzz is likely to make the original product even hotter by creating more customers, publicity, and new applications for the product. Consider Jibbitz, another company that has mastered this accelerated strategy, one that merits its own case study—and one that emphasizes that normal people who are immersed in normal daily activities can spot a seemingly simple idea that others have overlooked and turn it into big business. As with all the cases in this book, Sheri and Rich Schmelzer outsmarted the competition because they had vision. Sheri looked down at her daughters' Croc-shod feet and saw an unmet need.

JIBBITZ JEWELS

Similar to Grady, the entrepreneur best positioned for piggybacking might be an ultraloyal customer with a head for business. That's the Jibbitz story, too.

Sheri Schmelzer was the loyal customer. A stay-at-home mom in Boulder, Colorado, she was crazy about Crocs, the soft-resin clogs that mold to the wearer's feet for unusual comfort and have holes for air- and water-cooling at the beach. The runaway best-seller Crocs are made in Niwot, Colorado, a Boulder suburb, and carried by 1,600 retail outlets in 20 countries.

Sheri's husband, Rich, has a head for business. A serial entrepreneur, he founded and sold several software and Internet companies, including WorldPrints.com, a clearinghouse for art prints and desktop wallpaper. He sold the company in 2000 in a cash-and-stock deal worth an estimated $80 million.

ρ **Crocs**
To find out what's new, Peter Drucker advised us to keep walking in the marketplace. That's literally what the founders of Jibbitz did.

One day early in 2005, Sheri was working with her three young daughters on arts-and-crafts projects in the basement of their home. As usual, Crocs were scattered here and there—the family owned at least a dozen pairs. On a whim, Sheri stuck a silk flower through a hole in one of the clogs. She liked the effect, and so did her daughters. By the time Rich arrived home that evening, his whole family was wearing Crocs decorated with all sorts of baubles, including buttons and bows from a sewing kit. He took one look

© Crocs, Inc. Reprinted with permission.

and knew he had another winning business opportunity on his hands (or should I say feet?).

The Schmelzers had hitched their wagon to a fast-rising star. The unlikely stampede to buy the odd-looking Crocs has been spurred on by the clogs' comfort, their appeal to iconoclastic young buyers, and celebrity endorsements from the likes of Al Pacino and Faith Hill. But the success wouldn't have happened without shrewd business tactics on the part of Ron Snyder, the CEO that Crocs' founders brought in to run the business in 2004.

By then, Crocs were selling at a $13.5 million annual pace, up from just $1.2 million in their first year. But Snyder, who had run the global division of Flextronics, saw that as just the beginning. Sensing that Crocs could change colors and styles to match seasons and holidays, he revolutionized the shoe industry's antediluvian distribution model. Most shoe retailers must order their shoes in bulk and up to six months in advance. With Crocs, they can order as little as two dozen pairs and get them in just weeks. Snyder also decided to buy the Canadian manufacturer who made the shoes and owned the formula for the special resin that gives the clogs their comfort, feel, and odor resistance.

With sales continuing to mushroom, Snyder added manufacturing capacity. He wasn't thinking small, either; before long, plants in China, Italy, Mexico, and Romania were churning out Crocs. And the fad roared on. Worldwide sales in 2005 jumped to $108.6 million. The next year, sales nearly tripled to $322.2 million. In 2007, they were on pace to reach $446 million. Seventy colleges have ordered Crocs in their school colors, and branded Crocs have been made for companies ranging from Google and Tyco to Flextronics and the Los Angeles Lakers. Disney has ordered Crocs with Mickey Mouse–shaped holes. And just in case the fad should fade, Crocs has for sale or in the works 32 models to tempt fickle customers with new styles and combinations.

But Crocs was still in its relative infancy when Rich Schmelzer came home and saw the ornaments his wife and children had made for their clogs. He saw the potential in a flash. "It was such an obvious idea," Rich explains. "My kids were playing with them, and I thought, 'If my kids like it, every kid's going to like it.'" He wasted no time in patenting the idea, organizing a company, and coming up with a name for his wife's

ρ Jibbitz decorations
Riding someone else's market wave is tricky—the wave can crash. To mitigate that risk, the people at Jibbitz keep expanding their product line.

© Jibbitz, LLC. Reprinted with permission.

whimsy. Their company and decorations would be called Jibbitz, a homage to Sheri's nickname, Flibbertyjibbet.

The day after Sheri's fanciful invention, she went out and bought more durable ornaments—plastic peace signs and rhinestones—and glued them onto cufflinks that she then snapped into the holes in the Crocs. When the decorated clogs were ready, she sent them off to school on her daughters' feet. Their classmates took one look and clamored for some Jibbitz of their own. But Sheri still had a few kinks to work out—namely, making sure the Jibbitz could be inserted easily into (and removed from) the holes in the Crocs. Her seventh iteration proved to be the lucky design winner, a snap-in version that met her exacting standards.

To meet the budding demand created by their daughters' fashion-forward feet, Sheri and Rich set up a production line in the basement, charging $2.50 per Jibbitz. But as news of the decorations spread through Boulder, the multiplying orders forced them to move the operation to an office and hire some help.

On August 9, 2005, their wedding anniversary, the Schmelzers took Jibbitz online. "The web site just went crazy," Sheri recalls. "I was getting 200 to 250 orders a day." Then stores took notice of the market that was developing under their noses and began placing their own orders. The office gave way to a huge warehouse, and the manufacturing process was farmed out to a Chinese company.

The Jibbitz phenomenon, of course, was riding the bow wave of the giant Crocs fad, and more Crocs wearers were clamoring to decorate their shoes. Sheri was deluged with requests for new designs. Younger kids wanted their favorite cartoon characters, teenagers their favorite rock or rap stars. And Jibbitz's appeal was not limited to the young. "Hello Everybody," read a recent blog entry on the company's web site. "My name is Noortje, and I'm from Holland. Crocs are here very cool and for everyone, not just for kids! Mine are purple and today I've bought Jibbitz—four butterflies and two sunflowers. At the pediatrician where I work, the children like them very much. Love, Noor."

Sheri cranked out designs and Rich rode herd on the company's expansion. "We don't want to grow too fast," he told DailyCamera.com not long ago. "Organic growth and word of mouth is how we've been working." In other words, no advertising and, for a while, no orders from major retailers. He also wanted to make certain that, in the excitement of the product's popularity, operating efficiency didn't suffer. "We've failed if you call Jibbitz and we don't answer the phone," he says.

A smart businessperson, Rich had his eye on the company's future. He knew full well that piggybacking on a fad could last only as long as the fad itself. So even amid the mushrooming demand for Jibbitz-enhanced Crocs, he and Sheri were developing a new line of products, including wristbands, belts, anklets, and headgear—anything with holes that customers could insert their decorations into. As Sheri succinctly put it, "The more holes we have, the more Jibbitz we'll sell."

Eventually, the Schmelzers moved beyond products with holes to introduce a line of charms for cell phones and bracelets.

By summer 2006, the company had 40 employees. Jibbitz were being offered in 3,300 stores in the United States and hundreds more in Europe and the Middle East. More than six million pieces had been sold. "We couldn't be happier with Jibbitz's acceptance among consumers," Sheri announced in a company news release. "We have always wanted a creative, self-sustaining business that could give back to the community through the creation of jobs in Colorado and abroad."

Jibbitz was coming up roses, but a whole Pasadena Rose Bowl parade was heading the Schmelzers' way.

One hot day that summer, seven-year-old Lexie Schmelzer wore her Jibbitzed Crocs (what else?) to the local swimming pool, where a man walked up to her and presented his business card. "Have your Mommy call me," he urged her. The man was Duke Hanson, one of the three founders of Crocs, and Sheri called to chat. One thing led to another, and on October 3rd, Crocs announced its purchase of Jibbitz for $10 million in cash.

Jibbitz has since become a subsidiary of Crocs, with Rich Schmelzer as president and Sheri as chief design officer. The agreement stipulated they could earn up to $10 million more if Jibbitz met certain earnings targets, and they are well on their way to meeting those goals. They now have 1,100 products available, including a wide range of Disney-themed Jibbitz, from Mickey to Winnie the Pooh to *Pirates of the Caribbean* characters, plus all the mascots of the National Football League and the National Hockey League.

And it all came about because of Sheri's imagination and Rich's opportunistic eye for tapping the success of others and riding the Crocs' groundswell to fame and fortune.

GET SMART

> ▶ *You can have too much of a good thing.* Sometimes a market will respond so fast to your good idea that you don't have enough time to build the necessary delivery capability without risking a sacrifice in quality. In fact, I have found that almost all fast-growing companies outsell their delivery capabilities. But you can get in trouble if you sell too far ahead. Pacing is critical.

IN FACT, I HAVE FOUND THAT ALMOST ALL FAST-GROWING COMPANIES OUTSELL THEIR DELIVERY CAPABILITIES. BUT YOU CAN GET IN TROUBLE IF YOU SELL TOO FAR AHEAD. PACING IS CRITICAL.

Rich Schmelzer had the right idea, maintaining a disciplined growth pattern for Jibbitz. Like all entrepreneurs, he found it hard to resist the temptation to grow too fast; it's a heady feeling when orders are pouring in. After all, sales are the lifeblood of any business. But Rich understood that without the infrastructure to handle potential demand efficiently, he had to limit his commitments to customers.

If you're too busy to answer the phone, or if you can't maintain product quality or ensure on-time delivery,

you're going to lose customers no matter how popular
your product. They will simply give up on your ability to
satisfy their demands, opening the way for competitors to
steal your turf. Nothing, whether it's supply, demand, or
anything else, should prevent you from formulating and
then following a sustainable business model.

▶ *Think big.* As you build your business model, make sure it
is scalable. From the beginning, Jibbitz's growth potential
was limited only by the soaring growth of Crocs itself, but
not all new ventures are so lucky. People send me ideas
for new businesses almost every week. But only about 10
percent of them will ever produce a scalable business,
either because the market is not large enough to support
the idea or because the business has not been designed to
grow. The software-company ideas I get are particularly
susceptible to this failing.

▶ *Don't neglect your infrastructure.* It's critical that your
company's IT infrastructure and business processes
be able to handle increased volume without incurring
substantial added costs or needing to add people just to
maintain or improve service quality. All the companies
I researched for this book started with a lean attitude;
Jibbitz held its payroll to just 40 employees even as it grew
in overseas markets and outsourced production to China.

That said, the temptation to add people as you grow is
always there, especially if you start to incur operational
problems. In my reengineering work, I found that
throwing people at problems was often a company's first,

albeit ill-conceived, course of action. It's a nonsolution that often makes problems worse and substantially increases operating costs.

IN MY REENGINEERING WORK, I FOUND THAT THROWING PEOPLE AT PROBLEMS WAS OFTEN A COMPANY'S FIRST, ALBEIT ILL-CONCEIVED, COURSE OF ACTION. IT'S A NONSOLUTION THAT OFTEN MAKES PROBLEMS WORSE AND SUBSTANTIALLY INCREASES OPERATING COSTS.

Keep your organizational structure simple; that way, if you do need to add people, you can do it easily. Also, keep making sure your business model will be able to handle demand when you are ten times the size you are today. That way, you can't ever be blindsided when demand begins to heat up.

▶ *Think targeted marketing.* One way Rich Schmelzer kept operations under control was by relying on word-of-mouth marketing and Jibbitz.com; he avoided spending on traditional advertising. It pains me when I see so many young companies waste their cash on ad campaigns that make no sense at that point in their history.

I watched in disbelief during the dot-com bubble as companies spent foolishly on advertising. It proved the business adage that too much money—in this case, usually venture capital funds—saps your IQ. These not-smart companies believed they could advertise their way to quick product adoption even though their ideas were too new or too radical.

Those who tap the success of others don't have an adoption problem. The high-flying companies on whose shirttails they are riding have already created an immediate market for their product. Even so, you might feel an urge to tell the world about the other guy's product. That's understandable, but suppress it; you can use many other techniques today to bring your product and company to the attention of the people you need to reach.

▶ *Take the long view.* When you're in the midst of trying to make your business succeed, every waking hour is devoted to it, and it's hard to step back and think about the midterm future—not tomorrow or next week, but the next year or two. Yet it's an absolute necessity if you are to have any chance of long-term survival. Sheri and Rich Schmelzer understood that. Even as they were trying to cope with the runaway success of their Crocs decorations, they were planning Jibbitz product extensions into anklets, wristbands, and cell phone charms.

The good times won't roll forever. Eventually, the public tires of your product, competitors commoditize it, or, worse, they come up with a better version. Piggybackers are particularly vulnerable because their fortunes are riding on another company or product that might stumble or fall. If Crocs had worn out their welcome, the Schmelzers' diversification could still have given them a viable, if much-reduced, business. When Crocs purchased Jibbitz, the dynamic changed somewhat, but the point still holds.

QUESTIONS TO ASK YOURSELF

▶ Have you bought any popular products lately that seemed to cry out for an accessory or service that isn't available? Is this something that you could design, make, and sell?

▶ If your piggyback product or service proves popular, is the product you're hitched to doing well enough to give you a growing market?

▶ Are its makers likely to resent your piggybacking? Can you present your product or service as an item that makes the host product even more popular?

▶ What similar products can your add-on be used with?

▶ What other possibilities are the host product's makers neglecting to capitalize on? Can your product or service grow naturally into a whole line?

▶ However fast the host product is growing, can you control your own growth well enough to forestall loss of quality, chaotic delivery performance, and loss of customers?

▶ Thinking ahead, what will you do when growth of the host product slows down? Can your product be modified for other uses, or can you branch out to related products and services that you can sell without piggybacking on anything else?

THE YEAR IS 2001, AND YOU'VE
JUST SPENT $3,000 ON A NEW BIG
SCREEN TELEVISION SET. YOU'VE
INVITED ALL YOUR FRIENDS OVER
TO WATCH THE SUPER BOWL IN A
FEW DAYS AND SHOW OFF YOUR
SUPERCLEAR PICTURE—AND NOW
YOU'VE LOST THE REMOTE. YOU
RUN TO THE STORE WHERE YOU
BOUGHT THE SET. THEY TELL YOU
TO CONTACT THE DISTRIBUTOR OR
THE MANUFACTURER. EITHER WAY,
IT'S GOING TO TAKE A COUPLE OF
WEEKS OR MORE BEFORE YOU GET
A NEW REMOTE.

CHAPTER 8

Compete by Creating Order Out of Chaos: Partsearch Finds the Item You Need

You can just hear the laughter as you crawl around the floor pushing buttons on the set.

Back then, the business of providing replacement parts for consumer durables was a disaster area. Customers were unhappy, and retailers either didn't care or didn't know what to do about the problem. There was no way they could keep thousands of parts from dozens of manufacturers on hand, and that meant customers had to jump through hoops to order the items they needed (What's the part number? What's the model number on the machine?) and then wait endlessly for them to arrive.

Enter Dean Summers and Glenn Laumeister. Summers managed a chain of retail electronics stores, and he was all too familiar with the routine, which almost always left his customers frustrated and angry enough to go somewhere else for their next purchase. Laumeister was a veteran entrepreneur and marketer, a specialist in applying technology to solve complex business problems.

ρ **TV remote**

Did you know that your television remote is one of 8 million available parts and accessories—all with different part numbers—carried by PartSearch? Organizing a complex market is a big—and challenging—business opportunity.

Together they created an enterprise that would bring order and sanity to the chaos that was the parts business. They called it Partsearch Technologies.

From day one, Partsearch was dedicated to helping retailers, repairmen, and consumers thread through a maze containing literally millions of parts. It was a market that had never bothered to organize itself; every manufacturer's parts list was configured differently. So Partsearch developed a catalog in which each model of home appliances, electronic goods, and the like was presented with a list of all its parts. Obvious, right? Yet it had never been done before.

Today the Partsearch catalog lists eight million parts and accessories for more than 560 brands covering consumer electronics, major appliances, wireless devices, and outdoor power equipment. Its clients include Best Buy, Circuit City, Radio Shack, and CompUSA. And it's not limited to retailers: Individual consumers, manufacturers, and service shops turn to Partsearch for help. In 2006, the company had revenues of $63.7 million—plus an astounding compound annual growth rate since 2001 of 85 percent. And it all happened because a couple guys recognized the opportunity presented by a chaotic market.

When the two founders connected in fall 2000, Laumeister was an entrepreneur in residence at the New York incubator of Idealab, a Pasadena, California, business dedicated to creating and operating pioneering technology companies. The timing was not ideal. Laumeister's world was reeling from the dot-com crash—an event, incidentally, that he had predicted after being visited by a pair of Yale sophomores who had $1 million to spend and wanted Idealab's advice on starting an incubator.

In contrast to the vague dreams of many such dot-com high-flyers, Laumeister found the concept of Partsearch intriguing, he told me, "because it was a very straightforward, down-to-earth business where the customer is actually happy that they've interacted with you." Of course, making it happen was another matter. The problem was simple enough to describe, but the solution turned out to be more than a little complex.

Some industries, like automobiles, were out of bounds from the start because the manufacturers themselves made a profit from the aftermarket, selling parts and accessories for their products. But the supply chain for manufacturers of consumer durables was more fragmented, and what they really cared about was building products and getting them sold, period. They would be delighted if someone could free them from the messy business of providing parts for repairs and servicing what they had built. Clearly, the big manufacturers and their retail outlets would be ideal partners for Partsearch.

Laumeister decided to concentrate on two target markets: service professionals trying to repair appliances and electronic equipment, and individual consumers. In the latter group, the focus would be on those who had the skill and patience to make their own repairs, people who could take apart a dryer and replace a faulty heating element. The company's call center or web site would answer any questions either group might have about obtaining or installing a part.

⌕ **TV repair shop**

Partsearch is inclusive—it is designed for consumers and repair people alike and is both high-tech and high-touch.

⌕ **Best Buy**

Sometimes you need partners. Choose them carefully. Best Buy brought both channel and industry expertise to Partsearch.

Early on, Laumeister discovered that most manufacturers had their own individual and often impenetrable ways of organizing their parts information. On their parts lists, for example, the number for a particular part was not always matched with the model number of the product it fit into. Laumeister was determined to make Partsearch easy for customers to use, so he set about persuading the manufacturers to help by providing their parts lists. His goal was a system that would allow a visitor to easily search online for a Sony KV27 model, for instance, and see all its parts come up in a comprehensible list that would make it easy for customers to choose the gizmo they needed.

It was a several-year process, however, just to get manufacturers to provide their data and then to figure out how to standardize and present it. The Partsearch idea was new, and Laumeister had a hard time convincing

manufacturers that helping to create an efficient, consumer-friendly parts supply chain was worth their time. Finally, he sold a few retailers on the notion, and they, in turn, pressured manufacturers to get onboard.

The breakthrough partner was Best Buy, which sells technology and entertainment products and services in more than 900 stores in the United States and Canada. Before the Partsearch era, a Best Buy customer who needed to replace the battery in a laptop computer had to fill out a service tag in the store and leave the computer there. The machine was sent to another location for servicing and eventually was returned to the store, which then had to call the customer to arrange a pickup. So the customer had to make two trips to the store and do without the computer for as long as two weeks, and Best Buy had to pay for the shipping costs and the time spent by employees—all to replace a battery.

Best Buy was ready to hand over the whole process to Partsearch, but not before putting Laumeister and his people to the test: They had to have a workable parts-retrieval system up and operating within four weeks, or Best Buy would give the job to someone else.

Since Partsearch had barely opened its doors for business when Best Buy threw down the gauntlet, everyone had to scramble to make the deadline. A parts database had to be created from scratch, and because the manufacturers weren't cooperating, Partsearch had to rely on data from distributors and wholesale suppliers. "We had this database guy who worked like 20 hours a day, drinking Starbucks, never showering or shaving—just

ρ Laptop
Technology will continue to proliferate. Some business models will require the ability to handle scale and increasing complexity. Getting to a market first with scale can be a critical competitive advantage.

putting all that stuff into the catalog," Laumeister recalls. "Of course, he was being paid by the hour, so he was real happy."

As an added complication, credit cards couldn't be handled online in those days, so Partsearch had to cobble together a transaction-processing system with an old, unused phone system, and had to hire a call center to take customers' card numbers. In the end, when Partsearch sold $500 in parts the first day and the system was up and running, Laumeister was even happier than his database technician.

Now when Best Buy customers need a battery for a computer, they simply order it, either at a kiosk in a Best Buy store, using the Best Buy toll-free number, or at Bestbuy. com. Partsearch receives and fulfills the order in a matter of days. (Laumeister and his people never touch a part; the Partsearch business model relies on the manufacturer or his supplier to actually retrieve an ordered part, package it, and ship it to the customer.) The customer simply unpacks the battery

and installs it in the laptop herself—with help, if needed, from a sympathetic counselor on a live phone line. As far as the customer is concerned, it's Best Buy taking care of her needs—and doing so quickly and accurately. Partsearch handles Best Buy's returns and exchanges in the same unobtrusive way.

An analysis of the arrangement's financial benefits for Best Buy over a five-year period indicates that the company realized a net benefit of more than $11 million—saving almost $40 million in costs while paying Partsearch $29 million. In addition, Best Buy took in an estimated $1.2 million of extra revenue attributed to purchases from a more loyal customer base. And that's not all: Having access to the Partsearch catalog means that Best Buy's technical repair staff no longer has to search through web sites, file cabinets, and three-ring binders for technical data, greatly increasing its productivity.

Now that Best Buy and other major retailers have signed on and Partsearch has built a substantial customer base, only a few manufacturers continue to withhold their parts lists from Partsearch. "It's become a competitive thing," Laumeister told me. "Manufacturers see that if customers can get great data on the other companies' products through us, but their own data is weak, it reflects badly on them. They want to make sure they're as good as or better than anyone else because what they have on our site is part of their brand."

When Partsearch finally gets a manufacturer's parts list, the challenge is to make it fit into the Partsearch catalog so that a customer with, say, a defective DVD player need only enter the brand and model number to locate the parts needed to fix

it. Some manufacturers organize their lists by the function of
the parts, placing all amplifiers, for instance, in one section,
regardless of whether they're for TVs, DVDs, or CD players.
Other manufacturers have separate sections for each electronic
device, but the parts for all the models in each category are
listed together. Some give no clue which model a part fits into.

To work through the maze, Partsearch and a partner in India
have devised a process for taking apart all the lists and putting
them back together again, with each model listed separately
and all its parts automatically viewable online by a customer
who enters the brand and model number. "In many cases, we
had to create data that didn't exist before," says Laumeister. In
fact, they were creating order out of chaos.

Partsearch has applied advanced information technology
to reinvent the process of ordering and fulfillment, thus
making sense of a market that had been running badly on
automatic. And because products and parts keep proliferating,
the company has to keep updating both its catalog and its
information technology, requiring an investment of about $5
million a year.

Almost from the start, Partsearch's rapid growth forced
Laumeister to spend much of his time in pursuit of new
financing. Idealab had made a small initial investment, but
then came the dot-com crash, and most risk capital dried
up. The drought intensified after the terrorist attacks of 9/11.
After knocking on dozens of doors, Laumeister decided that
the venture capitalists were like a bunch of kids standing at
the edge of a cold creek. They found the company and its new

business model enticing, but no one wanted to be first to jump in. Laumeister told me, "Finally, I just told a guy, 'Listen, if you're going to do it, then it has to be now because we're going to be out of business in three months.'" The fellow signed on. Within a week, Laumeister was deluged with calls from other venture capitalists clamoring to be included.

Providing parts may sound like a simple, straightforward mission, but many customers find ways to make it complicated. Seeing no added value in the basic order-taking process, Laumeister's strategy calls for orders to be handled automatically over the web, and he is constantly tweaking the site to make it simpler and more efficient. At the same time, he trains the company's call-center employees, located in Ulster, New York, about 90 miles north of New York City, to cope sympathetically and intelligently with customers who don't quite know what they're doing. As such, the call-center transactions add value. (As you might have noticed, Partsearch joins other fast-growing companies in this book that focus on humanizing their call-center operations and minimizing the voicemail that so infuriates customers. It's a lesson well worth remembering.)

Here's how the call center works: A television repair person calls the center from a customer's home, for example. He can't fix the customer's television set because he doesn't have the part he needs, nor does he have a parts list or manual at hand. He asks if the call-center employee can help him find the part number and order it. By the end of the call, the repairman knows the part will arrive at his place of business in three days, which allows him to schedule another appointment on the spot instead of playing telephone tag with the customer. Now the repairman has a reason to order additional parts from Partsearch, and his customer might be more likely to buy another appliance from a retailer whose repairman is so efficient.

When a handyman consumer calls and is unsure of which parts he needs for a repair, the call-center representative can access the product's service manual and guide the caller through the repair process, suggesting which tools and auxiliary parts might be needed for the repair in question. This kind of interaction is simply another example of how high-tech problems still require the human touch.

Sometimes consumers order the wrong part, Laumeister told me. "But the reps are trained to spot that," he says, "especially when an order is atypical. A little flag goes up, and the rep asks if the caller is sure it's the right part and what he or she wants to do with it. That saves customers a lot of trouble. "

In the company's training presentations and other communications, employees are continually reminded of how their jobs fit into the organization as a whole and how they are helping people. The message Laumeister wants to get across is this: Finding parts sounds boring, but it's really about simplifying the lives of people just like you.

Laumeister also devotes a lot of thought and energy to finding the right kind of people for the call center and then motivating them. To staff all of Partsearch's operations, he looks for men and women who are easy to get along with and who have an appetite for success. He believes his employees come to work for three reasons: to make a living, enjoy interacting with their fellow workers, and be a part of a successful, worthwhile organization. To that end, Laumeister shares every success—whether it's a positive customer reaction or the acquisition of a new client—with everyone in the company. "Winners like to win," he says. "We post letters from happy customers on the wall and send e-mails around if someone in any part of the company has done something special. We have a lot of enthusiasm around here."

Laumeister's overarching vision for his company is nothing less than to become "the glue that holds the whole parts business together." When Partsearch first appeared as a blip on the screen of this antiquated, fragmented industry, such a goal would have seemed laughable. Not anymore.

GET SMART

> ▶ *Choose the right chaos to tame.* Dysfunctions exist everywhere, with chaotic conditions that can make life miserable. But there's no point in trying to tackle a problem if you bring no special resources to the table.

> Laumeister's background was in creating and operating high-tech companies, and he knew how to use information technology to solve complex problems. Fixing the dysfunctional, disorganized parts market was a challenge suited to his skills. He wouldn't have dreamed, for instance, of trying to cure sick airlines, with

their endless delays, overbooking problems, cattle-car conditions, and passengers infuriated by interminable waits on runways. But someday, someone who knows the airline business will conquer that chaos and profit hugely from it. Maybe it will be you.

▶ *Look for fragmentation.* If you have an appetite for a strategy that's based on simplifying complexity, look for an industry that has a lot of fragmentation. In the research for this book, I was struck by how many companies have been launched just to help patients negotiate the mazelike healthcare industry. Finding a new television remote might not have the same life-or-death aspects as treating an illness, but the problem for consumers is the same: No one has created an integrated set of services to quickly respond to a customer need. Fragmented industries—those in which there are many operating parts that do not work well together—provide some of the best opportunities for high-growth strategies.

FRAGMENTED INDUSTRIES—THOSE IN WHICH THERE ARE MANY OPERATING PARTS THAT DO NOT WORK WELL TOGETHER—PROVIDE SOME OF THE BEST OPPORTUNITIES FOR HIGH-GROWTH STRATEGIES.

▶ *Go for scale.* Although mastering complexity in a fragmented industry is required, it might not be sufficient to outsmart your competitors in the long term. Others might be able to quickly copy your approach. But if you can achieve scale early in the development of your business, just as Partsearch did, you can become the resource of choice. (This strategy is similar to what you read about earlier in Chapter 2, "Compete by Seeing What Others Don't: How Sonicbids Spotted a $15 Billion Market.") The combination of ease of access, almost unlimited choice, and competitive pricing is hard to beat.

THE COMBINATION OF EASE OF ACCESS, ALMOST UNLIMITED CHOICE, AND COMPETITIVE PRICING IS HARD TO BEAT.

▶ *Overcome inertia.* At two turning points in the life of Partsearch, Laumeister met resistance and found ways to overcome it. Resistance is a given at every kind of startup. The song says that no one loves you when you're old and gray, but in the business world, being young is a drawback, too. Manufacturers wouldn't cooperate with Partsearch until retailers pressured them, so Laumeister found a way to begin his catalog without the manufacturers and let Best Buy take the lead in converting them. Venture capitalists hemmed and hawed until Laumeister gave an ultimatum to one of them. But once he landed one backer, they all wanted to shower Partsearch with money. These kinds of obstacles seem as needless as they are difficult and infuriating, but be prepared for them. And if you can't get around them, find another line of work.

A heavyweight partner can make a business launch easier, as Partsearch demonstrated, but you risk being overwhelmed—or overtaken—by your partner. Before Laumeister sought help, he had already developed a capability that could not be easily or quickly replicated. And because he was adding value to his partners' businesses, he had a better chance of being treated fairly in a deal. The lesson here is to develop a unique and valuable capability before you seek a partner to enter a market. You will be taken more seriously, and you will be better able to protect your own interests.

THE LESSON HERE IS TO DEVELOP A UNIQUE AND VALUABLE CAPABILITY BEFORE YOU SEEK A PARTNER TO ENTER A MARKET. YOU WILL BE TAKEN MORE SERIOUSLY, AND YOU WILL BE BETTER ABLE TO PROTECT YOUR OWN INTERESTS.

> ▶ *Expect and look for more complexity.* When Laumeister started out with Partsearch, his goal was to make it easier for customers to find a part. Things got more complicated when he realized that some customers were ordering the wrong parts for the job they wanted to do. He could have ignored their confusion, chalking it up as just another example of human frailty. Instead, he trained his call-center representatives to be on the lookout for such callers and to help them order correctly. That response furthered Laumeister's overall goal of profiting and growing by helping people live their lives with less trouble and expense. In today's world, a businessperson had better enjoy dealing with complexity; it's here to stay.

> ▶ *Pair value with values.* The desire to run a business that actually helps people might sound a bit Pollyanna-ish, but Laumeister had it right. There's something liberating and

inspiring about a business that makes a real contribution to society, not just for the owners and leaders, but for employees and customers as well. And those feelings translate into an upbeat, can-do culture; a loyal workforce; happy customers; outstanding profits; and a spectacular growth rate.

QUESTIONS TO ASK YOURSELF

- ▶ Do you have the appetite for dealing with complexity? Do you enjoy making sense out of chaos?

- ▶ Can you find a fragmented industry or fragmented part of an industry that can be tamed?

- ▶ How will you begin to tame the beast?

- ▶ Can you find an approach that will enable you to deal with scale and more complexity, while offering more options over time?

- ▶ How fast can you scale the business?

- ▶ Can you create a sense of purpose that is strong enough to bring people to your cause?

- ▶ Can you break into the business or industry alone, or will you need partners?

- ▶ Have you gone far enough in developing your ideas and business so that you have some leverage in negotiating with your partner?

HERE'S A TALE OF SHEER, UNNECESSARY CORPORATE COMPLEXITY THAT IS WORTHY OF *THE GUINNESS BOOK OF WORLD RECORDS.* A MONTH OR SO AFTER THE APPLE IPHONE WENT ON THE MARKET, FOLLOWING ONE OF THE BIGGEST PRODUCT BUILD-UPS EVER, CUSTOMERS BEGAN RECEIVING THEIR FIRST SERVICE BILLS FROM AT&T.

CHAPTER 9

Compete by Simplifying Complexity: SmartPak Brings Stability to the Stables

For Justine Ezarik, a graphic designer in Pittsburgh, it was a shockingly memorable experience. Her bill came not in an envelope, but in a box—all 300 pages of it. Each of her Internet communications was listed, one by one. It was an example of corporate complexity run amok that AT&T isn't likely to forget, either. Ezarik posted a video on YouTube showing her opening the box and inspecting the bill, one page at a time. To keep the length of the clip down to about a minute, some of the paging is speeded up to a near blur of hands and paper. Within a few days, 100,000 people were laughing and shaking their heads over AT&T's gaffe. Sometimes complexity kills.

This chapter features an enterprise that taught me a great deal about simplification. It's built on a down-to-earth technique for taking the complexity out of caring for four-legged creatures and easing the minds of the people who love them.

HORSE SENSE AT SMARTPAK

Paal Gisholt was never much for horses. The venture capitalist likes to call himself "a notable nonrider." However, he is happy to allow his marketer wife, Becky Minard, to indulge the equine addiction she has had since childhood—especially now that her hobby of riding and raising horses has led the two of them to a profitable business proposition.

Together Minard and Gisholt have built SmartPak, a business dedicated to horses, health, and simplicity. By creating preselected, premeasured, and prepackaged medications and supplements for individual horses, and shipping them out in

⌖ Paal and Becky

Like the founders of DLI and Jibbitz, Becky was a consumer who saw a need and, with her husband, Paal, brilliantly built a business around it.

daily dosing packets, the pair has removed all the complexity that used to prevent animals from regaining or maintaining health.

The idea for the company came to light in 1999. That's when Minard, who had been riding horses since she was 10, purchased a horse named Westley for herself and her two daughters. And though Westley was notably undernourished and suffering from an eye ailment that could cause blindness, Minard was smitten. She knew that all he needed was a lot of love and attentive care.

Minard's veterinarian confirmed that Westley would recover fully if he received a daily regimen of food supplements and other drugs. But on an inspection tour of the horse farm where Westley boarded, Minard discovered, to her shock, that the horse hadn't been getting his prescribed supplements.

© SMARTPAK. Reprinted with permission.

The barn manager explained that the 30 horses under his care each required an average of three different supplements each day, and owners sometimes favored particular brands. So at feeding time, more than 100 tubs of pellets or powders had to be opened, the correct quantity for each particular horse scooped out, and the tub resealed. Getting it done at all was hard. Getting it done right 100 percent of the time, he said, especially with minimally skilled labor, was so complicated it was virtually impossible.

After talking with other horse owners and managers, Minard realized that the problem was common and widespread. Awkward-to-use supplement tubs invited dosage miscalculations—some animals would get too little, others could be harmed by getting too much. Worse, the need to juggle all those

ρ **Horse barn**

SmartPak's products are for horses. Now, Becky and Paal are expanding to dogs. Could people be next? You bet, but how will the healthcare industry respond?

containers caused some to be spilled and others to be left open. Too often the product that remained was exposed to air, sun, moisture, and pests—even mold and mildew. No wonder some horses seemed never to get their strength and spirit back after an illness. To a horse lover like Minard, this was absolutely unacceptable.

Upon boarding Westley at his home stable, Minard began working with the stable staff to ensure that not just her horse, but all the horses received their proper allotment of daily supplements and medications. Knowing that day-of-the-week pill containers help people track their drugs and dosages, Minard set out to design something similar for horses. What resulted was an easy-to-open plastic container with multiple wells, each containing the correct quantity of powders or pills, and labeled with the horse's name. It was exact—and, better yet, it was easy. Any stable hand, no matter how busy or untrained, could do the job right the first time.

When Minard talked with Gisholt about launching a business based on her invention, he was enthusiastic. Using her skills as a marketer and his as a venture capitalist, they got to work. They further honed the packaging concept, came up with a name for their invention (SmartPak), and began raising the money needed to start production.

SmartPak.com was launched in June 2000. Today the couple presides over a nationwide $40 million business that encompasses nutritional supplements and gear for dogs as well as horses. The company's volume is soaring—up 46 percent in 2006 alone.

Minard and Gisholt have achieved outstanding business success by finding an ingenious way to simplify complexity. But I'm not just talking about their product; the company is organized in a way that avoids many of the complications that plague older, more hidebound operations.

When I first heard about SmartPak, I thought it would be an old-fashioned, down-on-the-farm operation—a horse-and-buggy business, if you will. I was wrong. It turned out to be an example of a smart enterprise at its best, with customized products, in-depth customer service, subscription-based deliveries, and, underpinning it all, sophisticated information technology.

None of this came into being right away, of course, and innovating to this extent surely isn't easy. But being smart and capable of spotting opportunities to simplify has paid off handsomely for SmartPak. Nevertheless, as Gisholt reminded me, "You also pay a price to grow a market all by yourself." He got advice from Minard and some knowledgeable mentors, but he still had to figure things out as he went along.

ρ **SmartPak products**
Some new business models require no new product technologies—just an intelligent way to package and deliver what already exists.

© SMARTPAK. Reprinted with permission.

To satisfy customer preferences, SmartPak stocks 300 different products, each of which is available in three dosage sizes. To take the planning and worry out of the long-distance purchase of supplements, the company ships its customers a four-week supply of SmartPaks 13 times a year—a sort of book of the month club for animals. Orders can be placed through SmartPak.com, where visitors can compare and contrast different brands, or through a printed catalog, which some customers find more to their liking. In addition, customers are invited to contact the SmartPak call center for all sorts of equine advice, not just product information.

You might assume that all of this customization and individualized service comes at a premium price, but SmartPak has found ways to stay competitive with the companies that supply supplements the old-fashioned way, in buckets. How have Minard and Gisholt managed to do it? One of the best ways to keep prices down, they realized, was to hold shipping costs down. It's hard to do when you're shipping lesser quantities more often than your competitors. But Gisholt went to UPS with a simplification proposition that the shipping company couldn't refuse.

"We figured that if we could create a master account structure and have shipments for a whole bunch of different customers coordinated, it would save UPS a ton of money," Gisholt told me. With SmartPak's help, the UPS truck making, say, 20 different delivery stops a month to hand over 30 separate packages of supplements is now able to make the same deliveries in just two stops. Just as Gisholt had hoped, UPS gave SmartPak the break on shipping rates it needed to hold down prices. As Gisholt explained with a shrug, "UPS shared back some of its savings with us, and we shared back some of our savings with the customer."

Still, Gisholt and Minard realized that their efforts to hold down prices would fail even with a money-saving shipping agreement if they didn't somehow address the matter of customization. Typically, companies tack on an additional charge for providing products in single units rather than in bulk. Labor costs force them to charge even more for customized packaging of the sort SmartPak specializes in. Once again, they devised a persuasive argument to bring to the startup's suppliers.

Gisholt went to the manufacturers and pointed out that the SmartPak system helps ensure customer satisfaction because the horse owners receive the freshest and most exactingly measured products. In addition, the steady, monthly pulse of SmartPak shipments makes supplier production planning easier and smoothes out a supplier's revenue stream. "We convinced the suppliers there would be a substantial amount of incremental income for them because of our autoship mode," Gisholt says, "and they have shared some of those gains with us." Of course, once SmartPak grew to be one of the largest buyers of supplements in the world, the company enjoyed even greater price leverage.

Now SmartPak views its suppliers as part of the team. Some, in fact, have formalized the relationship, entering into exclusive partnerships with SmartPak. These select suppliers receive previously unavailable information—vital statistics such as sales trends and market penetration—all courtesy of

SmartPak's state-of-the-art information technology system. Manufacturers know what's being shipped where, and which of their products are being used with another company's product. Gisholt says that kind of transparency enables them to "make better decisions about the segments of the market where they're having traction and where they should focus their investments."

Gisholt and Minard have wisely paid close attention to customer service, too. SmartPak uses the Internet almost exclusively to reach out to present and potential customers, and also to receive and manage customer orders. Three out of four orders are handled online. To handle that fourth order and other customer-service issues, Gisholt and Minard established a call center manned

© SMARTPAK. Reprinted with permission.

by extremely well-qualified people, most of whom are degreed experts in animal or equine science. Each call center advisor undergoes extensive training and is then given—what else?— free rein.

SmartPak's call-center employees have come to be regarded as the horse world's wise men and women, but it took a concerted effort to gain that trust. Before the horse community found SmartPak, SmartPak found the horse community—and introduced itself. Call-center employees surfed the web in search of sites and message boards pertaining to horse care, posting answers and suggestions whenever they could. They also encouraged advice seekers to follow up by phone with SmartPak, well aware of the marketing opportunities. The callers' contact information was entered into the company's database, helping to create a list of potential customers.

SmartPak's call center is now considered the place to go whenever a horse owner has a problem. Callers know that whether the issue is dietary or behavioral or something else, SmartPak employees will take the time and make the effort to find a solution. They also appreciate that no one is looking over the call-center staffer's shoulder with a stopwatch. This kind of generous and open attitude builds trust and, not incidentally, loyalty. "The horse community is relatively small and tight," Gisholt told me. "There are a lot of message boards and chatter that goes on. Our people on the phones get talked about all the time. They're heroes every day, and I think they're responsible for a large portion of our growth."

It is hardly simple or easy to set up a full-service call center like SmartPak's. But Gisholt and Minard accepted the complexity involved in operating such a call center and spent the time needed to work out their various systems, in the sure knowledge that their efforts would simplify life for their customers. Had they chosen to go lean on customer service, forcing customers to deal with long waits and less knowledgeable assistance, SmartPak would not be the company it is today.

The choice to invest in customer service is not problem free, of course. Advisors make mistakes. Customers get mad. Sticky situations have to be carefully unstuck. Gisholt takes the hassle in stride. When call-center employees mess up, Gisholt offers coaching. "We help them fine-tune their judgment over time and never hang them out to dry," he told me. Some of this fine-tuning happens one-on-one, but most of it is dealt with structurally. Customer problems are routinely entered into the SmartPak information technology system, most of which was developed internally. Each week Gisholt calls a "failure-to-meet-expectations meeting" that includes senior representatives from the IT department, the call center, and fulfillment functions, as well as some company officers. They review every instance of customer disappointment, whether through a shipping foul-up, miscommunication, or poor advice. They then come up with systems—electronic ones, wherever possible—to prevent the mistake from happening again.

"We use information technology for every single thing we can," Gisholt told me, "not just to improve productivity, but to lift our quality and prevent error." For example, the company developed a machine that uses an electric eye to test whether a SmartPak package moving along the conveyor belt is full or empty; the information is then compared to the order info in the database to make sure they match up. If a package doesn't match the information in the database, the conveyor is automatically halted. All SmartPaks ready for shipping have a barcode, as does the paperwork for the shipment; both the package and the paperwork must be scanned and matched before a shipping label can be printed. It's a complex way to keep things simple.

I asked Gisholt if SmartPak had any direct competition. Because the company's equine-supplement business has a relatively small share of the market, it wouldn't be surprising to find other companies nipping at its heels. But rivals are few, Gisholt says, citing a number of factors that have tended to keep competitors at bay. SmartPak's wide range of products (it offers 80 percent of what's sold in the market) is one factor, along with the substantial technology investment required, the difficulty of raising capital, Gisholt and Minard's exclusive partnerships with suppliers, and the patent protection they have won for their packaging. Would-be competitors have to think long and hard before entering this niche, and that's no accident, Gisholt assured me. "We're trying to force them to run to catch a moving train," he says, while throwing up blockages wherever possible.

Logistics are part of
almost every business. But
companies can't always
afford to develop these
capabilities on their own.
The good news: Lots
of competent business
partners are available
to help.

GET SMART

▶ *Don't just cut your own costs.* Too often,
companies are so busy looking for ways
to cut costs within their own operations
that they don't think to do the same
for their suppliers. That way, they miss
out on a major opportunity to improve
their own financials. SmartPak made it
easy for UPS to significantly reduce its
deliveries of equine supplements and
provided manufacturers with all sorts of
market advantages, through previously
unavailable market information. It
solved some of their headaches and
simplified their operations. Both parties
showed their appreciation by reducing
their prices for SmartPak.

Helping suppliers reduce costs also
means that suppliers will remain
healthy and competitive. Michael
Dell knew that when he developed

Dell's build-to-order business model. If you need to draw quickly on the material and services of suppliers, you need suppliers that are healthy and competent.

But working with suppliers for your joint benefit requires adherence to three principles: standardization, transparency, and trust. Both you and your suppliers have to develop a set of shared business processes so that information and materials will move freely between your organizations. When managing complexity, you want to maintain it only in areas important to your business model—just as Gisholt and Minard have done with customer service. Simplify and standardize everything else, especially processes involving suppliers.

To work more efficiently with your suppliers, you must be more transparent about your operations. It's the only way to jointly solve problems and prevent breakdowns. Transparency, in turn, requires a common trust that each of you is acting in the others' interest and that you both will benefit from the operational changes a new business model generates.

To work more efficiently with your suppliers, you must be more transparent about your operations.

- ▶ *Beef up your culture.* Gisholt and Minard first choose horse-smart call-center people, then they train them, and, finally, they give them a chance to make decisions on their own and learn from their mistakes. In addition to providing terrific customer service, that approach creates a cadre of enthusiastic, loyal employees. Gisholt puts it this way: "If you have a strong culture, you don't need all those controls." By "all those controls," he means instructing employees on what to do in every conceivable circumstance, thus taking away their initiative, and penalizing them if they stray. That's a recipe for unhappy employees, sky-high turnover, and bad customer service.

GISHOLT PUTS IT THIS WAY: "IF YOU HAVE A STRONG CULTURE, YOU DON'T NEED ALL THOSE CONTROLS."

Can a strong culture continue to do without controls and rules when a company branches out to multiple locations, different cities, and possibly other countries? Certainly, as your company gets larger, you need to find ways to discern what's going on and to make sure people are behaving as your business model requires. But avoid any rules and controls that prevent people from taking intelligent action. Before putting rules and controls in place, try articulating a set of principles about how people in your company are expected to behave, and make it clear that there will be no tolerance for violating those principles. If the principles are high minded, they will not appear as a threat, but rather something to which everyone can aspire.

▶ *Develop an appetite for technology.* If ever there was a company committed to leveraging technology in the service of simplicity, it's SmartPak. I mentioned its use in such areas as production and quality control, but you can see it underpinning virtually every aspect of the operation—for example, inventory turns that are so speedy with the help of IT that they have substantially trimmed the company's capital needs.

It's possible to look at information technology today and argue that, because it has become ubiquitous, it is not key to your competitiveness. Everyone has equal access to the Internet, but how you use technology can make your business model unique when it is combined with superb business processes. You must look at technology and processes together, constantly asking how IT can help your processes improve, especially in the way in which your customers experience them. It's the combination of technology and process that makes SmartPak's strategy exceptional.

QUESTIONS TO ASK YOURSELF

▶ Can you identify where value will be created for your customers by simplifying their lives?

▶ Can you spot any complexity within your industry that can be managed for the benefit of your customers?

▶ Are there ways that you and your suppliers can collaborate to your joint benefit and profits—and for the benefit of your customers?

▶ Are you prepared to standardize nondifferentiating processes?

▶ Are you prepared to be more transparent with your
  suppliers? Are your suppliers prepared?

▶ Can you establish a level of trust with your suppliers that
  will enable joint problem solving?

▶ Can you establish a strong culture so that you can predict
  how your people will behave, to minimize controls?

▶ How strong is your appetite for information technology?

▶ Is your technology enabling you to improve your business
  processes?

AS I WARNED IN CHAPTER 1,
"IT'S A SMART, SMART, SMART,
SMART WORLD," THE ACTIONS
OF THE COMPANIES PROFILED
IN THIS BOOK DON'T LEND
THEMSELVES TO ANY HARD-
AND-FAST FORMULAS YOU
CAN FOLLOW TO GUARANTEED
SUCCESS. BUT THERE ARE
CERTAINLY DIFFERENCES
BETWEEN THE SMARTEST
COMPANIES AND THE
"INCUMBENTS" THAT OPERATE
IN TRADITIONAL WAYS.

EPILOGUE

And those differences suggest some general lessons that smart leaders in every line of business can apply. Here are a few of them:

> ▶ *Ambition matters.* Companies that outsmart the competition look for dramatic growth, while incumbent businesses are content with incremental growth. And as with a winning baseball team, you can achieve dramatic growth by knocking the ball out of the park or by pecking away with a string of singles that drive runs in. The companies in this book look for both home runs and a constant string of base hits.

COMPANIES THAT OUTSMART THE COMPETITION LOOK FOR DRAMATIC GROWTH, WHILE INCUMBENT BUSINESSES ARE CONTENT WITH INCREMENTAL GROWTH.

A small-to-medium company with a great strategy and good execution skills can double or even triple in size every two to three years. That kind of growth would be difficult, if not impossible, for a big business simply because of scale. There's no denying that scale can be a real drag on percentage growth, but sometimes it becomes an excuse for not growing.

That said, there's more to growth than outsize percentage gains. Growth is about ambition. Smart large corporations like Procter & Gamble, for example, also outgrow their rivals, and all companies—both large and small—that outsmart their competitors exude excitement and a sense of purpose that feeds their appetite for growth and further reinforces their ambition.

GROWTH IS ABOUT AMBITION.

The problem with incumbent companies is that their more precise, formal, risk-averse management styles can suck the oxygen and excitement out of the air employees breathe. They smother ambition rather than fuel it. At large incumbents, new products or services might initially have a small impact on the existing business, so they attract little attention, are starved for resources, or are rigidly controlled. Consequently, the proponents of new ideas lose their ambitious outlook. Ideas die.

▶ *Intuition reigns.* Companies that outsmart the competition make strategic choices based largely on intuition, whereas incumbent businesses often get bogged down in research and analysis.

COMPANIES THAT OUTSMART THE COMPETITION MAKE STRATEGIC CHOICES BASED LARGELY ON INTUITION, WHEREAS INCUMBENT BUSINESSES OFTEN GET BOGGED DOWN IN RESEARCH AND ANALYSIS.

Incumbent organizations spend inordinate amounts of time looking at market data and the performance of competitors. Planning takes on a life of its own, management gets professionalized, and decisions get compromised by committees sure to include skeptical viewpoints. Intuition is frowned upon, and the courage of leadership is drowned in the soothing waters of safe harbor analysis. It becomes easier to decide to do nothing, to stagnate.

As noted in Chapter 1, the companies in this book follow Peter Drucker's strategic advice to figure out where you are today, where you want to be in the future, and how to get there. But they don't spend a lot of time analyzing the impact of their actions. They are guided by the intuition of their founders and leaders, most of whom have either substantial industry expertise or the right sensibilities and skills for the job ahead.

These companies continuously test ideas in the market and are adept at using the Internet to gauge customer response. For smart companies, the Internet is a boon that allows them to quickly and directly canvass customers to see what they think. In large incumbent companies, though, the sales force, the marketing department, and other structures can get in the way and prevent leaders from knowing what customers really think. And once fantasy replaces reality, even good intuition is useless.

▶ *Focus prevails.* Businesses that outsmart their competitors stay focused on what they do best, while incumbent companies are often searching for new ideas and end up losing their sense of purpose in the process.

BUSINESSES THAT OUTSMART THEIR COMPETITORS STAY FOCUSED ON WHAT THEY DO BEST, WHILE INCUMBENT COMPANIES ARE OFTEN SEARCHING FOR NEW IDEAS AND END UP LOSING THEIR SENSE OF PURPOSE IN THE PROCESS.

As smart companies grow, they have to find new ideas for products and services to feed growth just as incumbent companies do. But companies that outsmart the competition stay focused on the customers and markets they know. They build on their knowledge, testing variations and enhancements to existing products or services. Even if they have thousands of product offerings, they typically remain focused on a well-defined customer need.

That's not so with incumbent companies. Having lost touch with their original purpose, these businesses might be so desperate for growth that they will foolishly move to markets they don't really understand. Very successful incumbents might also become arrogant and, believing they can do anything, plunge into ventures they are neither suited for nor capable of carrying off. They soon lose their way.

▶ *Customers rule.* Companies that outsmart competitors focus on how they can better serve customers; incumbent companies focus on their competitors.

COMPANIES THAT OUTSMART COMPETITORS FOCUS ON HOW THEY CAN BETTER SERVE CUSTOMERS; INCUMBENT COMPANIES FOCUS ON THEIR COMPETITORS.

I have been struck by just how attuned to customer needs these fast-growing businesses seem to be. Often they are built on a simple idea, perhaps to solve a problem shared by friends. Yet they never lose their connection to their customers. Their new products and services grow out of a continuing, almost fanatical focus on solving a customer problem. They are looking straight ahead at the customer and do not allow themselves to be led astray by peripheral market noise.

Incumbents, on the other hand, often become distracted in their search for growth opportunities by what competitors are doing. In working with such organizations, I have seen too many strategy documents that focus on the analysis of competitors rather than on the needs of customers. Maybe it's because incumbents fear their competitors or think their rivals have discovered a better way forward. What they don't understand is that meaningful strategic differentiation depends not on competitors, but on the needs of a company's customers.

▶ *Calm enables.* Companies that outsmart the competition accept risk as a normal part of doing business. For incumbents, risk drives decisions and hampers progress.

COMPANIES THAT OUTSMART THE COMPETITION ACCEPT RISK AS A NORMAL PART OF DOING BUSINESS. FOR INCUMBENTS, RISK DRIVES DECISIONS AND HAMPERS PROGRESS.

Leaders of high-growth businesses might be facing life-and-death situations every day, but they don't even think about it. Their passion overrides their fear. Just the opposite is true at risk-wary incumbents, where leaders allow fear to override their passion.

In every one of my interviews with the executives featured in this book, I asked what mistakes they had made in growing their companies. With rare exception, they appeared flummoxed by the question or said they had never focused on their mistakes. All told me that they were always learning and saw mistakes as a natural process in the development of their companies. For them, accepting risk is the normal way to do business, and they don't fear making mistakes. Rather, they think about how to recover and learn from mistakes when they happen.

Incumbents, by contrast, are always aware of potential risk. If they are publicly held, they worry that their shareholders won't easily forgive their mistakes. And that worry might not be misplaced, even though risk-taking often proves to be in shareholders' best interest. I believe the shortsightedness of shareholders prevents many incumbent companies from doing what they need to do to grow. That's why so many publicly held companies are looking at going private, so that they can take necessary risks out of the public's sight.

I BELIEVE THE SHORTSIGHTEDNESS OF
SHAREHOLDERS PREVENTS MANY INCUMBENT
COMPANIES FROM DOING WHAT THEY NEED TO DO
TO GROW.

> ▶ *Innovation lives.* Companies that outsmart their
> competitors have a culture that values and freely
> promotes innovation. Incumbents subject innovation to a
> cumbersome process.

COMPANIES THAT OUTSMART THEIR COMPETITORS
HAVE A CULTURE THAT VALUES AND FREELY
PROMOTES INNOVATION. INCUMBENTS SUBJECT
INNOVATION TO A CUMBERSOME PROCESS.

In all the interviews for this book, no one used the word
innovation, but everyone was searching for new ideas and
getting the good ones into the market as soon as possible.
Some of the smartest companies I know do have processes
in place to vet new ideas, but they are highly supportive—
acknowledging and thanking people for their creativity,
even if the ideas are impractical. In fact, innovation is a
cultural marker of the companies in this book.

Incumbents, however, throw up roadblocks to creativity
by overintellectualizing and overdesigning innovation
processes. Desperate to find the key to growth, they
establish processes to search for new ideas inside and
outside their companies. But unless they allow for true
freedom of action, they can end up stymieing people
with an innovative bent. I am not necessarily critical

of innovation processes; they can yield good ideas. But innovation must be deeply embedded in a company's culture and encouraged at every turn. Otherwise, even good ideas will die. People commit themselves to innovation only when the actions of a company consistently acknowledge its importance.

BUT INNOVATION MUST BE DEEPLY EMBEDDED IN A COMPANY'S CULTURE AND ENCOURAGED AT EVERY TURN.

▶ *Culture drives.* Companies that outsmart their competitors depend on culture to manage behavior. Incumbents use rules and controls.

COMPANIES THAT OUTSMART THEIR COMPETITORS DEPEND ON CULTURE TO MANAGE BEHAVIOR. INCUMBENTS USE RULES AND CONTROLS.

In my conversations with people at the companies featured in this book, I noticed that everyone seems to know just what to do at key moments—a customer emergency, a transgression by an employee, or some other breakdown. Shared values and beliefs drive and control behavior. Sometimes these bedrock values are made explicit; sometimes they are undeclared and simply appear in time of need. In either case, they lead people to the right solution.

In incumbent businesses, especially big ones, rules and controls often dominate, and they sometimes seem to insult the intelligence and integrity of the organization's employees. The prevailing assumption is that, when given the chance, people will do the wrong thing—exactly the opposite view of companies in this book.

▶ *Everyone plays.* Companies that outsmart the competition engage all their people in constructing and executing strategy, whereas, at incumbent organizations, strategy is often an abstraction for most people.

COMPANIES THAT OUTSMART THE COMPETITION ENGAGE ALL THEIR PEOPLE IN CONSTRUCTING AND EXECUTING STRATEGY, WHEREAS, AT INCUMBENT ORGANIZATIONS, STRATEGY IS OFTEN AN ABSTRACTION FOR MOST PEOPLE.

So often in incumbent companies, employees don't understand the corporate strategy. It's dictated from the top. The people who are excluded are left to wonder what this year's big idea will be and how it will affect them. So rather than pitch in to help shape the company's direction and performance, they grow passive and listless. Strategy becomes an abstraction—something to be feared, not embraced.

In talking with people at every level of the smartest companies I know, it's clear that they all believe they own a piece of the solution. Because these companies look for

ᴏ **Jim Champy**
With a nod to Nike, whose slogan put it best, my advice is: Just do it. Good ideas are rare and precious.

distinctiveness in almost everything they do, opportunities abound for everyone to get involved, whether it be contributing ideas or executing them. The inclusiveness also nurtures a company's growth because everyone sees himself or herself as a partner in setting strategy, not a minion being imposed upon from on high.

The question all these comparisons raise is whether incumbent businesses can adapt and learn to behave as smart companies do. The answer is yes. Witness the amazing example of Smith & Wesson, described in Chapter 4, "Compete by Using All You Know: Basics Are Blazing at Smith & Wesson." Remember, though, that change begins with identifying where you want be in the future and changing your behavior accordingly.

Author Photo: Rodney Smith

And on another note, when you look at your own organization, you might well find other lessons from some of the companies portrayed in this book. They have a great deal to teach all of us, and I don't pretend to have mined every ounce of their collective wisdom.

I want to leave you with one final precept that every leader of these smart companies would endorse. With a nod to Nike, whose slogan put it best, my advice is: Just do it. Good ideas are rare and precious. When one turns up, grab it and go with it. Make sure it's really in your line of business and meets your customers' needs, but don't dwell too long on what could go wrong. Just do it. If it turns out to be a mistake, learn from it and do something else. The point is to always be inclined to action.

Now go out there and outsmart your competitors.

A

accessories, market for, 114-122, 125

accumulated wisdom, importance of, 61

affiliations, 88

AltaVista, 83

ambition, growth and, 165-166

AOL, 89

Apple, 16

AT&T, 147

auto industry, 91, 117

B

Bain Capital Ventures, 45

Baum, Dan, 81, 89

Berklee College of Music, 24

Best Buy, 135-137

Black & Decker, 66-70, 77

INDEX

H

I

S